Celtic Cross-Stitch

Mike Vickery

Sterling Publishing Co., Inc. New York
A Sterling/Chapelle Book

For Chapelle Limited

Owner: Jo Packham

Editor: Leslie Ridenour

Staff: Malissa Boatwright, Sara Casperson,
Rebecca Christensen, Holly Fuller, Amber Hansen,
Holly Hollingsworth, Susan Jorgensen, Susan Laws,
Amanda McPeck, Barbara Milburn, Pat Pearson,
Cindy Rooks, Cindy Stoeckl, Ryanne Webster,
Nancy Whitley and Lorrie Young

Photographer: Kevin Dilley for Hazen Photography

Special thanks to Kerry O'Neal of The Irish Gift House
in Tempe, Arizona for her valuable consultation.

If you have any questions or comments or would like
information on specialty products featured in this book,
please contact:

Chapelle Ltd., Inc.
PO Box 9252
Ogden, UT 84409
Phone: (801) 621-2777: FAX: (801) 621-2788

Bibliography

Cirker, Blanche: *The Book of Kells: Selected Plates in
Full Color;* Dover, New York, 1992.

Davis, Courtney: *The Art of Celtia;* Blandford, London,
1994.

Davis, Courtney: *The Celtic Art Source Book;* Blandford,
London, 1988.

Delaney, Frank: *Legends of the Celts;* Sterling, New York,
1992.

Rutherford, Ward: *Celtic Mythology;* Sterling, New York,
1987.

Stewart, R.J.: *Celtic Gods, Celtic Goddesses;* Blandford,
London, 1990.

Library of Congress Cataloging-in-Publication Data

Vickery, Mike.
    Celtic cross-stitch / Mike Vickery.
        p.   cm.
    "A Sterling/Chapelle Book."
    Includes index.
    ISBN 0-8069-1382-7
    1. Cross-stitch–Patterns. 2. Decoration and ornament, Celtic.
I. Title.
TT778.C76V53 1996
746.44'3041–dc20   95-32938
                                                      CIP

10 9 8 7 6 5 4 3 2 1

A Sterling/Chapelle Book

First paperback edition published in 1996 by
Sterling Publishing Company, Inc.
387 Park Avenue South, New York, N.Y. 10016
© 1996 by Chapelle Ltd.
Distributed in Canada by Sterling Publishing
% Canadian Manda Group, One Atlantic Avenue, Suite 105
Toronto, Ontario, Canada M6K 3E7
Distributed in Great Britain and Europe by Cassell PLC
Wellington House, 125 Strand, London WC2R 0BB, England
Distributed in Australia by Capricorn Link (Australia) Pty Ltd.
P.O. Box 6651, Baulkham Hills, Business Centre, NSW 2153, Australia
Printed and bound in China
All rights reserved

Sterling ISBN 0-8069-1382-7 Trade
             0-8069-1383-5 Paper

The written instructions, photographs,
designs, patterns and projects in this
volume are intended for the personal use
of the reader and may be reproduced for
that purpose only. Any other use,
especially commercial use, is forbidden
under law without the written permission
of the copyright holder.

Every effort has been made to ensure that
all the information in this book is accurate.
However, due to differing conditions, tools,
and individual skills, the publisher cannot
be held responsible for any injuries, losses,
and other damages which may result from
the use of the information in this book.

mike vickery

Although interested in art from a young age, Mike did not begin his designing career until 1992. Dissatisfied with his career in the computer field, he quit and then began working for a cross-stitch company. Within a year he left the company and began working as a free-lance designer.

Becoming a free-lance designer allowed him to work from his home office and spend more time with his wife, Amy, and his two children, Justin and Maegan.

In his spare time, Mike enjoys jogging, music, sports, and gardening in the yard of his home in the foothills of the north Georgia mountains.

A talented fine artist as well, he is a member of the Etowah Arts Council. His fine art is on display at the Etowah Art Gallery in Cartersville, Georgia.

Mike was excited to be able to create the designs in this book. He was not familiar with Celtic art and enjoyed learning the history of this unique style. He appreciated the challenge of creating designs this rich, detailed and fascinating.

CONTENTS

BORDERS

LETTERS

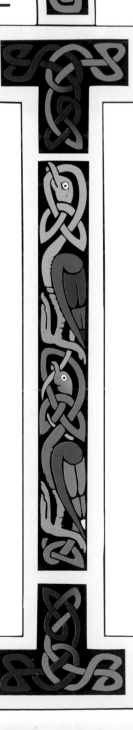

CONTENTS

LETTERS

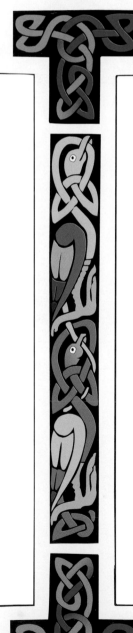

LEGENDS

Till the soil—bid cities rise—

Be strong, O Celt—be rich, be wise—

But still, with those divine grave eyes,

Respect the realm of mysteries.

William Sharp

sword style

Fabric
Aida 11
Aida 14
Aida 18
Hardanger 22

Design Size
2⅞" x 7½"
2¼" x 5⅞"
1¾" x 4⅝"
1⅜" x 3¾"

Stitch count: 31 x 83

Anchor			DMC	
			Step 1:	Cross-stitch
1	⊡	◿		White
886	☐	◿	677	Old Gold-vy. lt.
297	▨		743	Yellow-med.
323	▨	◿	722	Orange Spice-lt.
324	◉	◿	721	Orange Spice-med.
326	▦	◸	720	Orange Spice-dk.
48	☐	◿	818	Baby Pink
24	▨	◿	776	Pink-med.
27	▨	◿	899	Rose-med.
46	■		666	Christmas Red-bright
43	▨	◣	815	Garnet-med.
104	▨		210	Lavender-med.
87	▦		3607	Plum-lt.
159	⊞	◿	3325	Baby Blue-lt.
149	■	◣	311	Navy Blue-med.
185	▨	◿	964	Seagreen-lt.
186	▣	◿	959	Seagreen-med.
187	▨	◸	958	Seagreen-dk.
206	⊡		955	Nile Green-lt.
204	▨		912	Emerald Green-lt.
403	■		310	Black

			Step 2:	Backstitch
403	⌐		310	Black

In the latter third and second centuries B.C., the Celtic art form had become more asymmetrical compared to the previous Vegetal style. Vines, tendrils and lyre shapes were fitted with heads of dragons and other beasts. They were also given tails which added complexity to their shape.

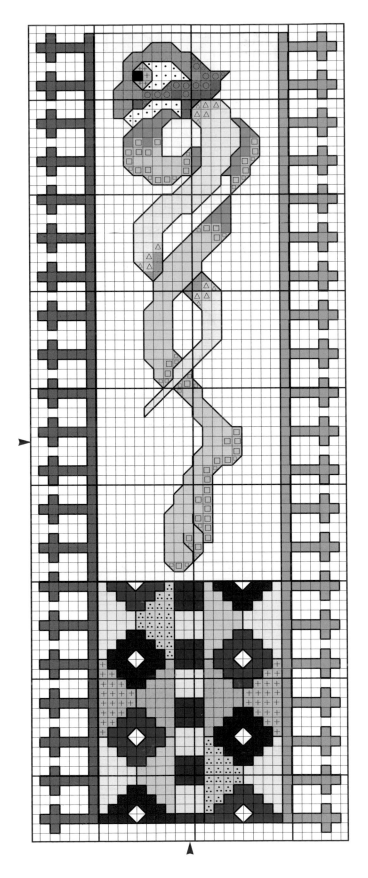

FRETTED

Fabric	Design Size
Aida 11	¾" x 8⅛"
Aida 14	⅝" x 6⅜"
Aida 18	½" x 5"
Hardanger 22	⅜" x 4⅛"

Stitch count: 8 x 90

Anchor		DMC	
Step 1:		Cross-stitch	
323		722	Orange Spice-lt.
324		721	Orange Spice-med.
326		720	Orange Spice-dk.
203		954	Nile Green
204		912	Emerald Green-lt.
228		910	Emerald Green-dk.

Anchor		DMC	
Step 2:		Backstitch	
403		310	Black

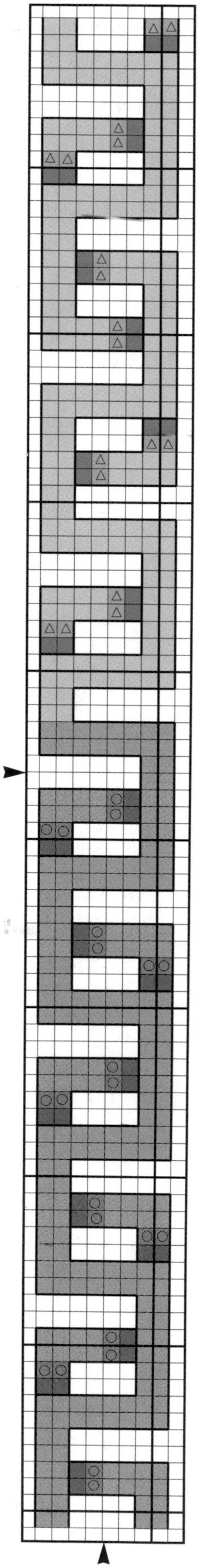

KNOTS & VINE

Fabric	Design Size
Aida 11	¾" x 2½"
Aida 14	⅝" x 2"
Aida 18	½" x 1½"
Hardanger 22	⅜" x 1¼"

Stitch count: 8 x 28

Anchor		DMC	
Step 1:		Cross-stitch	
87		3607	Plum-lt.
228		910	Emerald Green-dk.
204		912	Emerald Green-lt.
203		954	Nile Green
362		437	Tan-lt.
370		434	Brown-lt.

Anchor		DMC	
Step 2:		Backstitch	
403		310	Black

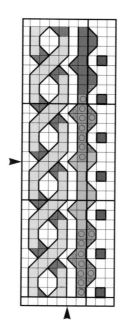

BIRD

Fabric	Design Size
Aida 11	1⅝" x 8⅛"
Aida 14	1¼" x 6⅜"
Aida 18	1" x 5"
Hardanger 22	⅞" x 4⅛"

Stitch count: 18 x 90

Anchor			DMC	

Step 1: Cross-stitch

Anchor			DMC	
1	⊡	◿		White
301	☐	◿	744	Yellow-pale
297	◉	◿	743	Yellow-med.
303	☐	◿	742	Tangerine-lt.
886	☐	◿	677	Old Gold-vy. lt.
323	▨	◿	722	Orange Spice-lt.
324	▲	◿	721	Orange Spice-med.
326	■	◿	720	Orange Spice-dk.
48	☐	◿	818	Baby Pink
24	R	◿	776	Pink-med.
27	▨	◿	899	Rose-med.
35	▨	◿	3705	Melon-dk.
46	■	◿	666	Christmas Red-bright
104	▨	◿	210	Lavender-med.
105	▣		209	Lavender-dk.
110	■	◿	208	Lavender-vy. dk.
87	▨		3607	Plum-lt.
159	▨	◿	3325	Baby Blue-lt.
145	⊞		334	Baby Blue-med.
132	■	◿	797	Royal Blue
185	☐	◿	964	Seagreen-lt.
186	⊠	◿	959	Seagreen-med.
187	■	◿	958	Seagreen-dk.
203	J	◿	954	Nile Green
204	▨		912	Emerald Green-lt.
228	▨	◿	910	Emerald Green-dk.
255	☐	◿	907	Parrot Green-lt.
256	G	◿	906	Parrot Green-med.
258	▨	◿	904	Parrot Green-vy. dk.
403	■	◿	310	Parrot Green-vy. dk.

Step 2: Backstitch

Anchor		DMC	
403	⌐	310	Black

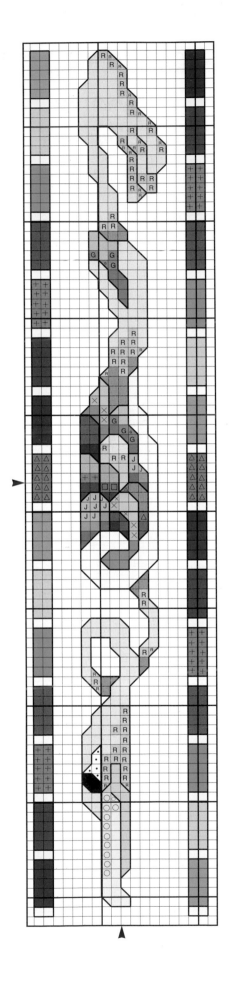

ORNAMENTAL

Fabric
Aida 11
Aida 14
Aida 18
Hardanger 22

Design Size
1" x 8⅛"
¾" x 6¾"
⅝" x 5"
½" x 4⅛"

Stitch count: 11 x 90

Anchor		DMC	
Step 1:		Cross-stitch	
297	☐	743	Yellow-med.
24	☐	776	Pink-med.
87	▦	3607	Plum-lt.
46	▦	666	Christmas Red-bright
43	▦	815	Garnet-med.
104	☐	210	Lavender-med.
159	◎	3325	Baby Blue-lt.
185	☐	964	Seagreen-lt.
149	▦	311	Navy Blue-med.
255	☐	907	Parrot Green-lt.
229	▦	909	Emerald Green-vy. dk.
357	▦	801	Coffee Brown-dk.
Step 2:		Backstitch	
403	⌐	310	Black
Step 3:		French Knot	
403	●	310	Black

Celtic ornamentation had three basic mediums: carving in wood and stone for personal and religious purposes; metal working in jewelry, domestic implements and battledress for trading to sustain the way of life of the chiefs; and in painting. The art was generally abstract and non-narrative, balancing form with delicate lines, bright colors and a myriad of spirals and interlacings.

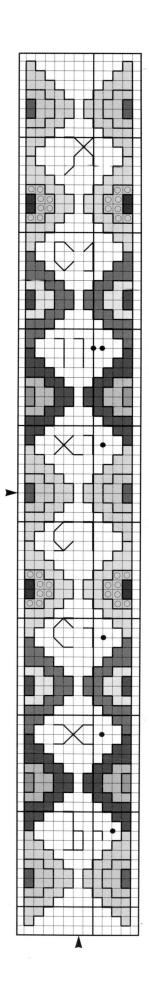

classic jewels

Fabric **Design Size**
Aida 11   1⅝" x 8⅛"
Aida 14   1¼" x 6⅜"
Aida 18   1" x 5"
Hardanger 22   ⅞" x 4⅛"

Stitch count: 18 x 90

Anchor			DMC	

Step 1: Cross-stitch

886	☐	◿	677	Old Gold-vy. lt.
891	✦	◿	676	Old Gold-lt.
297	☐	◿	743	Yellow-med.
323	▧	◿	722	Orange Spice-lt.
24	▨	◿	776	Pink-med.
35	▦	◿	3705	Melon-dk.
46	■		666	Christmas Red-bright
43	■		815	Garnet-med.
105	▦	◿	209	Lavender-dk.
159	▨	◿	3325	Baby Blue-lt.
149	■		311	Navy Blue-med.
186	⊞	◿	959	Seagreen-med.
204	▦	◿	912	Emerald Green-lt.
255	▨	◿	907	Parrot Green-lt.

Step 2: Backstitch

403	⌐	310	Black

The second and first centuries A.D. saw the increase of classical, or Roman, influence on Celtic works of art. The designs were more naturalistic and avoided the traditional plant forms. It is assumed that the craftsmen adapted their style to appeal to the taste of the foreign buyer.

Roman occupation stopped at Hadrian's Wall in Britain and Ireland was not absorbed into the Empire. However, through contact in trading, the Celts incorporated desirable aspects of Rome into their own culture.

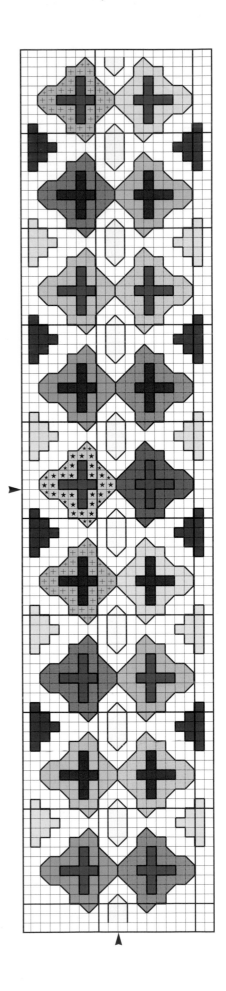

Kells

Fabric
Aida 11
Aida 14
Aida 18
Hardanger 22

Design Size
1½" x 6⅞"
1¼" x 5½"
1" x 4¼"
¾" x 3½"

Stitch count: 17 x 76

Anchor		DMC	
			Step 1: Cross-stitch
886	☐	677	Old Gold-vy. lt.
297	▨	743	Yellow-med.
46	◼	666	Christmas Red-bright
43	◼	815	Garnet-med.
159	◼	3325	Baby Blue-lt.
149	◼	311	Navy Blue-med.
203	◻	954	Nile Green
229	◼	909	Emerald Green-vy. dk.
357	◼	801	Coffee Brown-dk.

			Step 2: Backstitch
403	└─┐	310	Black

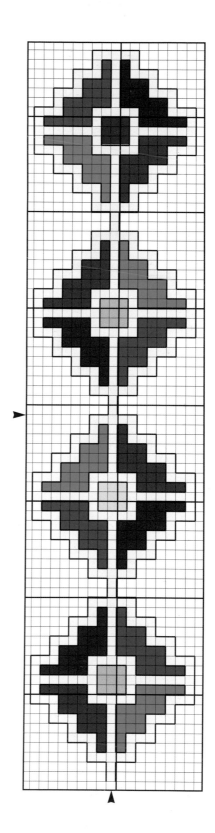

Fusion of Christianity with Celtic paganism after the the Roman departure around 140 A.D. produced major works of Celtic art. The Book of Kells is an illuminated manuscript which is believed to have been created in Ireland, northern England or Scotland around 800 A.D. Together with the Book of Durrow and the Lindisfarne Gospels, the three are definitive of the high level of skill and artistry of the period. These books were evangelistary, containing the four gospels in canon pages, carpet pages and text pages, and probably were intended for use as altar books.

serpents

Fabric

Fabric	Design Size
Aida 11	1¾" x 8¾"
Aida 14	1⅜" x 6⅞"
Aida 18	1" x 5⅜"
Hardanger 22	⅞" x 4⅜"

Stitch count: 19 x 96

Anchor			DMC	

Step 1: Cross-stitch

Anchor			DMC	
1	⊡	◿		White
891	⊞	◿	676	Old Gold-lt.
301	☐	◿	744	Yellow-pale
297	◉	◿	743	Yellow-med.
303	▨	◿	742	Tangerine-lt.
323	▨	◿	722	Orange Spice-lt.
324	▲	◢	721	Orange Spice-med.
326	■	◢	720	Orange Spice-dk.
48	☐	◿	818	Baby Pink
24	▣	◿	776	Pink-med.
27	▨	◿	899	Rose-med.
46	■	◢	666	Christmas Red-bright
43	■		815	Garnet-med.
87	■	◢	3607	Plum-lt.
105	▨	◢	209	Lavender-dk.
159	▨	◿	3325	Baby Blue-lt.
186	⊠	◿	959	Seagreen-med.
206	☐	◿	955	Nile Green-lt.
204	■	◢	912	Emerald Green-lt.
255	▨	◿	907	Parrot Green-lt.
256	▨	◿	906	Parrot Green-med.
258	■	◢	904	Parrot Green-vy. dk.
403	■	◢	310	Black

Step 2: Backstitch

403	└┐	310	Black

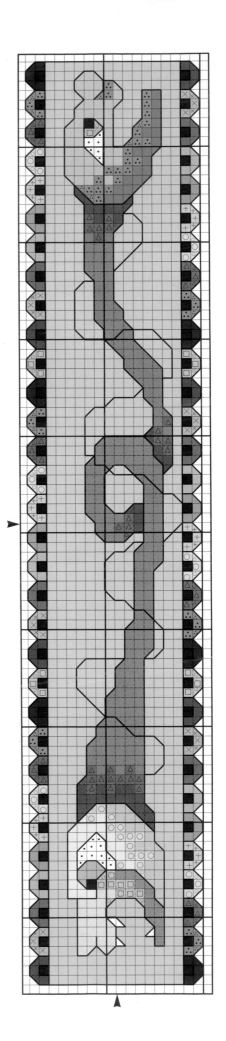

ṪHE CROSS

Fabric   **Design Size**
Aida 11   2½" x 8¾"
Aida 14   1⅞" x 6⅞"
Aida 18   1½" x 5⅜"
Hardanger 22   1¼" x 4⅜"

Stitch count: 27 x 96

Anchor			DMC	
Step 1:			Cross-stitch	
886	□	◿	677	Old Gold-vy. lt.
891	◉		676	Old Gold-lt.
890	▨	◿	729	Old Gold-med.
297	▨	◿	743	Yellow-med.
323	▨	◢	722	Orange Spice-lt.
326	▨	◢	720	Orange Spice-dk.
48	□	◿	818	Baby Pink
35	▨	◢	3705	Melon-dk.
46	■	◢	666	Christmas Red-bright
43	■	◢	815	Garnet-med.
159	▨	◿	3325	Baby Blue-lt.
149	■	◢	311	Navy Blue-med.
185	▨	◿	964	Seagreen-lt.
206	⬚	◿	955	Nile Green-lt.
203	⊞	◿	954	Nile Green
228	▨	◢	910	Emerald Green-dk.
255	▨	◿	907	Parrot Green-lt.
258	★	◢	904	Parrot Green-vy. dk.
362	▨	◿	437	Tan-lt.
370	▨	◢	434	Brown-lt.
Step 2:			Backstitch	
403	⌐		310	Black

Although representative of Christianity, the symbol of the Celtic cross is also viewed as four roads to eternity. The center circle is quartered to produce a wheel, which is often used as a symbol for the Sun, and the rule of Christ over all things encompassing length, breadth, height and depth.

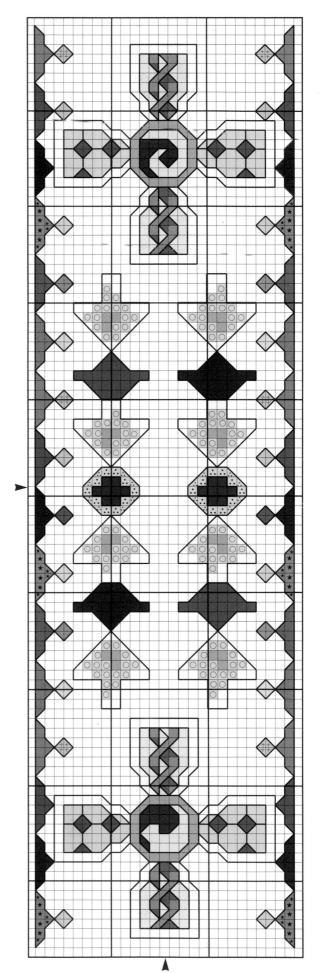

a

Fabric	**Design Size**
Aida 11	6¼" x 7¼"
Aida 14	4⅞" x 5¾"
Aida 18	3⅞" x 4½"
Hardanger 22	3⅛" x 3⅝"

Stitch count: 69 x 80

Ancestors of Anglo-Saxon peoples, the Celts first emerged around 1000 B.C. as a separate identifiable people in an area near the source of the Danube. They expanded into regions of central Europe, the Iberian peninsula, northern Italy, and into Polish Silesia, Bulgaria, Romania, Thrace, Macedonia, and western Turkey, where they were referred to as Gauls.

The arrival of the Celtic people in the British Isles is estimated to have been in 800 B.C. They were agriculturalists. Their staple was cereals and grains, grown for domestic consumption and exportation. There is evidence that they maintained deep storage silos, which were sunk into the ground and often lined with basketry. When new pits were dug, these were abandoned and used for rubbish.

Anchor			DMC	
Step 1:		Cross-stitch		
1	·	◿		White
301	⊞	◿	744	Yellow-pale
303	▨	◿	742	Tangerine-lt.
886	☐	◿	677	Old Gold-vy. lt.
891	▨	◿	676	Old Gold-lt.
890	K	◢	729	Old Gold-med.
24	⊠	◿	776	Pink-med.
27	S	◿	899	Rose-med.
75	☐	◿	604	Cranberry-lt.
76	▲	◿	603	Cranberry
78	■	◢	601	Cranberry-dk.
47	▲	◢	321	Christmas Red
43	■	◢	815	Garnet-med.
87	■		3607	Plum-lt.
89	◙		917	Plum-med.
104	☐	◿	210	Lavender-med.
110	■	◢	208	Lavender-vy. dk.
159	◻	◿	3325	Baby Blue-lt.
145	■	◢	334	Baby Blue-med.
134	●	◢	820	Royal Blue-vy. dk.
149	■	◢	336	Navy Blue
185	☐	◿	964	Seagreen-lt.
187	■	◿	958	Seagreen-dk.
206	U	◿	955	Nile Green-lt.
255	☐	◿	907	Parrot Green-lt.
258	■	◢	905	Parrot Green-dk.
862	■	◢	934	Black Avocado Green
362	☐	◿	437	Tan-lt.
370	■	◿	434	Brown-lt.

Step 2: Backstitch

403	└─	310	Black

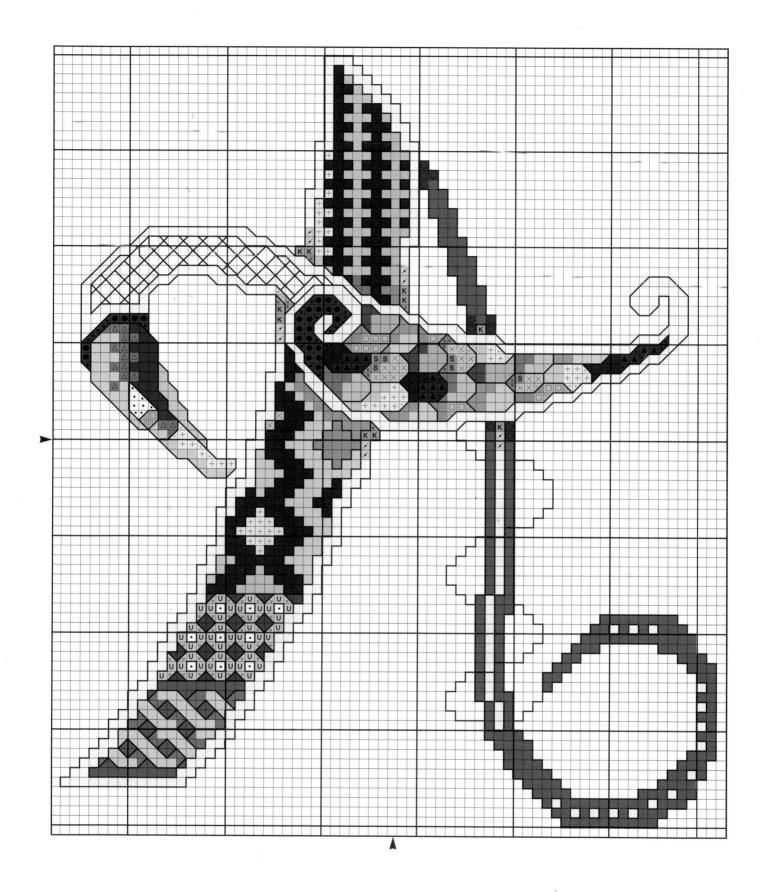

B

Fabric / Design Size

Fabric	Design Size
Aida 11	6⅛" x 6⅞"
Aida 14	5" x 5½"
Aida 18	3⅞" x 4¼"
Hardanger 22	3⅛" x 3½"

Stitch count: 70 x 76

Enjoying a great amount of prestige and reward, Bards played an integral role in Celtic society. They were the custodians of mythology—poets, musicians, storytellers. The Bards retained the character which is associated with that of a modern-day priest. They were respected as fonts of wisdom and took upon themselves the title "ollave," which means doctor or father.

By tradition, no requested gift could be refused a Bard. Should this occur, the Bard had the right to satirize the host.

Bards were free to cross tribal frontiers and were exempt from serving in the military. They retreated together in battle time and served as commentators on the game of war.

The Bard was expected to be well-versed in narrative and musical skills. Command of the Noble Harp Strains (the Lament strain, the Laughter strain, and the Sleep strain) was required.

The Arthurian Merlin is believed to have been based on a very accomplished Bard called Myrdinn.

Anchor			DMC	
Step 1:			Cross-stitch	
1	⊡	◿		White
886	☐	◿	677	Old Gold-vy. lt.
891	⊞		676	Old Gold-lt.
890	◼		729	Old Gold-med.
301	◸	◿	744	Yellow-pale
303	☐	◿	742	Tangerine-lt.
323	◼	◿	722	Orange Spice-lt.
326	◼	◢	720	Orange Spice-dk.
24	☐	◿	776	Pink-med.
27	◼	◿	899	Rose-med.
47	◼	◢	321	Christmas Red
43	◼	◢	815	Garnet-med.
104	◻	◿	210	Lavender-med.
110	◼	◢	208	Lavender-vy. dk.
87	◼	◢	3607	Plum-lt.
159	◻	◿	3325	Baby Blue-lt.
145	◼	◿	334	Baby Blue-med.
149	◼	◢	336	Navy Blue
185	▣	◿	964	Seagreen-lt.
187	◼	◿	958	Seagreen-dk.
213	◻	◿	369	Pistachio Green-vy. lt.
203	⊠	◿	954	Nile Green
204	◼	◿	912	Emerald Green-lt.
255	◻	◿	907	Parrot Green-lt.
258	◼	◿	905	Parrot Green-dk.
362	◻	◿	437	Tan-lt.
370	★	◿	434	Brown-lt.

Step 2: Backstitch

403	└┐	310	Black

Step 3: French Knot

403	●	310	Black

29

C

Fabric | **Design Size**
Aida 11 | 6⅜ x 6¾"
Aida 14 | 5" x 5¼"
Aida 18 | 3⅞" x 4⅛"
Hardanger 22 | 3⅛" x 3⅜"

Stitch count: 70 x 74

Cuchullain, legendary champion of Ulster, was called the most mighty warrior in the world and tired of continual challenges made by warriors of surrounding kingdoms.

He was the son of Lugh, who was a hero/god. Cuchullain is described as both sad and ferocious, with profound eyes akin to fire or gemstones the color of dragons' eyes, with a wide chest and as agile as a salmon leaping up a waterfall. His anger could grind an enemy to powder.

Cuchullain summoned forth incredible strength in what was called his "war tremors." When in this state, a drop of blood appeared on the point of each strand of his hair and seemed to blanket his pulsing skin.

Anchor			DMC	
Step 1:			Cross-stitch	
1	⊡	◸		White
886	⊠	◺	677	Old Gold-vy. lt.
890	◼		729	Old Gold-med.
301	◻	◺	744	Yellow-pale
297	⊡	◺	743	Yellow-med.
303	◻	◺	742	Tangerine-lt.
323	◼		722	Orange Spice-lt.
25	◼	◺	3326	Rose-lt.
42	◙	◺	335	Rose
35	◼	◺	3705	Melon-dk.
46	◼	◢	666	Christmas Red-bright
20	◼	◺	498	Christmas Red-dk.
44	◼	◢	814	Garnet-dk.
104	◻	◺	210	Lavender-med.
110	◼	◢	208	Lavender-vy. dk.
87	◼		3607	Plum-lt.
133	◼	◺	796	Royal Blue-dk.
185	◻	◺	964	Seagreen-lt.
187	◼	◺	958	Seagreen-dk.
213	◻	◺	369	Pistachio Green-vy. lt.
206	◿	◺	955	Nile Green-lt.
209	◼	◺	913	Nile Green-med.
205	◼	◺	911	Emerald Green-med.
942	◻	◺	738	Tan-vy. lt.
362	⊞	◺	437	Tan-lt.
309	◼	◺	435	Brown-vy. lt.
403	◼	◢	310	Black

Anchor		DMC	
Step 2:		Backstitch	
403	└─	310	Black

Fabric	Design Size
Aida 11	6⅜" x 6⅞"
Aida 14	5" x 5⅜"
Aida 18	3⅞" x 4⅛"
Hardanger 22	3⅛" x 3⅜"

Stitch count: 70 x 75

Children of the goddess Danu were among the first settlers on the island of Ireland. As spirits they traveled through the air and alighted on the land on the first day of May. The Dannans had powers of magic, which proved powerful and long lasting. They defeated the Fir Bolgs and the Formorians, who were horrible cyclopses. The Dannans ruled all of Ireland, except for one province, for many hundreds of years.

One day on the first of May, the sons of King Mil of Spain invaded the land and defeated the Dannans. The opposing sides made peace and divided the country between them. The sons of Mil, who became known as the Milesians and then the Celts, would rule all above the ground, and all under the ground was designated the rule of the Dannans. These spirits are believed to inhabit the underworld, still practicing magic.

Anchor   DMC

Step 1: Cross-stitch

Anchor			DMC	
288	□	◿	445	Lemon-lt.
301	⊠	◿	744	Yellow-pale
303	⊞		742	Tangerine-lt.
324	U	◿	721	Orange Spice-med.
886	□	◿	677	Old Gold-vy. lt.
891	◎	◿	676	Old Gold-lt.
890	■	◿	729	Old Gold-med.
48	□	◿	818	Baby Pink
868	■	◿	3779	Terra Cotta-vy. lt.
337	◪	◿	3778	Terra Cotta
27	■	◿	899	Rose-med.
42	■	◿	335	Rose
46	■	◢	666	Christmas Red-bright
43	■		815	Garnet-med.
87	■	◿	3607	Plum-lt.
98	▲	◿	553	Violet-med.
145	■	◿	334	Baby Blue-med.
170	■	◿	3765	Peacock Blue-vy. dk.
132	■	◿	797	Royal Blue
206	□		955	Nile Green-lt.
204	◻	◿	912	Emerald Green-lt.
187	▲	◿	958	Seagreen-dk.
258	■	◢	905	Parrot Green-dk.
246	■	◿	986	Forest Green-vy. dk.

Step 2: Backstitch

403	⌐	310	Black

Step 3: French Knot

403	•	310	Black

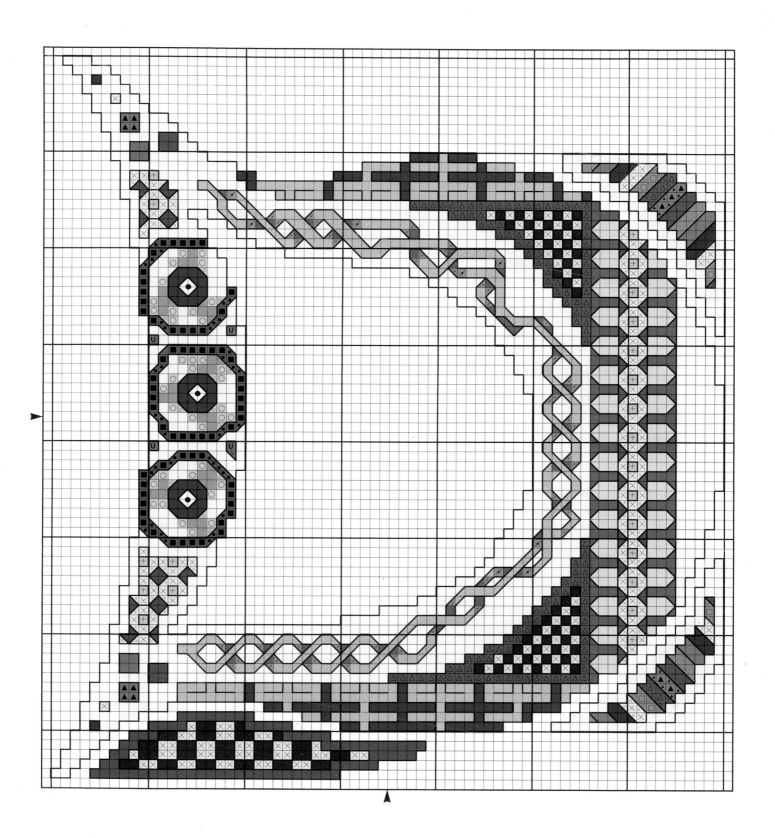

Fabric | **Design Size**
Aida 11 — 6⅛" x 6⅞"
Aida 14 — 4⅞" x 5⅜"
Aida 18 — 3¾" x 4⅛"
Hardanger 22 — 3⅛" x 3⅜"

Stitch count: 68 x 75

Considered to be the most beautiful woman in the Kingdom which belonged to Aengus, son of the magical King Eochy, Etain, who was the daughter of King Allil, was awarded to Midir for marriage. The two fell deeply in love.

However, Midir was already married. His jealous wife, Fuamnach, was a sorceress and cast a spell on Etain. She was then transformed into a purple butterfly. When Fuamnach saw that Midir loved Etain still, the delicate butterfly was caught up in furious never-ceasing winds.

Etain was finally rescued by Aengus, and, because of his magical powers, she was freed from the spell at nighttime. Aengus fell in love with her. The butterfly was again caught up in the winds and was, by mistake, ingested by a beautiful woman, who was the wife of the Hero Etar. Etain was transported to the womb of the woman and reborn as the daughter of the Hero Etar.

She grew gracefully into a young woman. While carrying out the duties of a normal day, she was noticed by a servant of Eochy. Eochy wooed and married her and she became the queen of Tara.

Midir found her again, told her of her history and convinced her to leave Eochy and enter with him into the Land of Youth. Years later, Midir returned to the angry Eochy and offered a replacement for Etain. Unknowingly, the woman Midir chose was his own daughter, who then bore him a child who sired a long line of heroes.

Anchor			DMC	
Step 1:	Cross-stitch			
1	⊡	◿		White
886	☐	◿	677	Old Gold-vy. lt.
891	◎	◿	676	Old Gold-lt.
890	◼	◢	729	Old Gold-med.
301	☐	◿	744	Yellow-pale
297	⊞	◿	743	Yellow-med.
303	☐	◿	742	Tangerine-lt.
323	◼		722	Orange Spice-lt.
48	☐	◿	818	Baby Pink
24	⊡	◿	776	Pink-med.
43	◼	◢	815	Garnet-med.
104	◼	◿	210	Lavender-med.
105	⊠	◢	209	Lavender-dk.
110	◼	◢	208	Lavender-vy. dk.
87	◼		3607	Plum-lt.
168	◼		518	Wedgewood-lt.
149	◼	◢	311	Navy Blue-med.
185	☐		964	Seagreen-lt.
213	☐	◿	369	Pistachio Green-vy. lt.
214	◺	◿	368	Pistachio Green-lt.
215	◼	◿	320	Pistachio Green-med.
246	◼	◢	319	Pistachio Green-vy. dk.
942	☐	◿	738	Tan-vy. lt.
363	☐	◿	436	Tan
373	☐	◿	422	Hazel Nut Brown-lt.
375	◼	◿	420	Hazel Nut Brown-dk.
944	◼	◢	869	Hazel Nut Brown-vy. dk.
403	◼	◢	310	Black

Step 2: Backstitch

403	⌐	310	Black

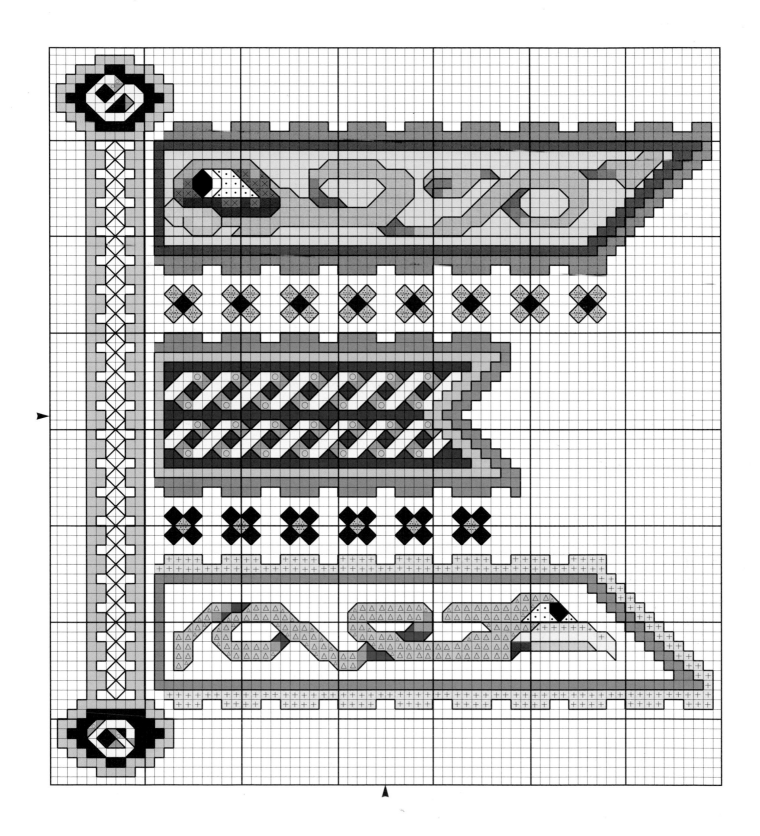

f

Fabric / Design Size

Fabric	Design Size
Aida 11	6⅜" x 6⅞"
Aida 14	5" x 5¾"
Aida 18	3⅞" x 4⅛"
Hardanger 22	3⅛" x 3⅜"

Stitch count: 70 x 75

*f*easting was definitive of a Celtic man's stature. A good host was judged by the size of his feast, the quality of the food, and the number and importance of the guests invited.

It was considered improper for a host or guest to begin discussing business until after the feast was completed. Some feasts were known to last three days or more.

The feast was the place where great matters were discussed and important decisions were made.

Bards (lyric poets and storytellers) and Druids (philosophers and theologians) were treated with respect and honor at the feast.

Anchor / DMC

Step 1: Cross-stitch

Anchor			DMC	
1	⊡			White
301	☐	◿	744	Yellow-pale
891	☐	◿	676	Old Gold-lt.
323	◼		722	Orange Spice-lt.
46	◼	◢	666	Christmas Red-bright
24	☐		776	Pink-med.
44	◼		814	Garnet-dk.
87	◼	◿	3607	Plum-lt.
105	◼	◿	209	Lavender-dk.
159	◎		827	Blue-vy. lt.
154	☐	◿	3755	Baby Blue
185	⊞		964	Seagreen-lt.
187	◼	◿	958	Seagreen-dk.
206	☐	◿	955	Nile Green-lt.
209	◼		913	Nile Green-med.
255	◻		907	Parrot Green-lt.
362	☐	◿	437	Tan-lt.
309	◼		435	Brown-vy. lt.
371	◼	◢	433	Brown-med.

Step 2: Backstitch

403	└─┐	310	Black

Step 3: French Knot

403	●	310	Black

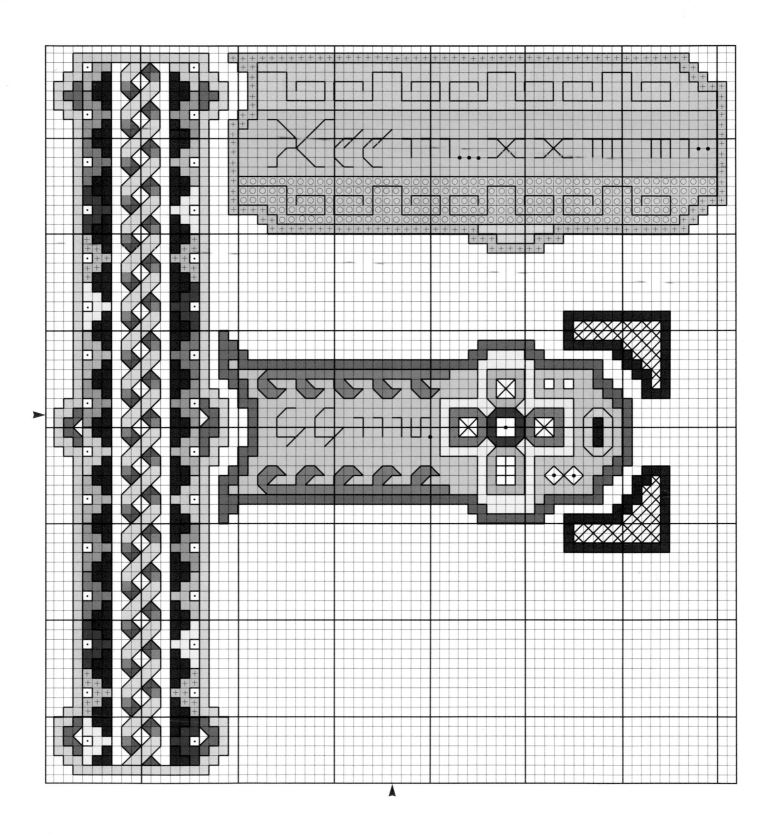

G

Fabric
Aida 11
Aida 14
Aida 18
Hardanger 22

Design Size
6⅜" x 7¼"
5" x 5¾"
3⅞" x 4½"
3⅛" x 3⅝"

Stitch count: 70 x 80

If a Bard was refused a requested gift or reward for a story or poem he delivered, he could sing the "glam dicin"—a terrible fate for the receiver. The song was a satirization of the character of the host. Shame and dishonor —and possibly death— would instantly fall upon his house.

Generally, this punishment was avoided at all costs and the bards fared well. The Welsh Bard, Taliessin, accrued 100 racehorses, 100 purple cloaks, 100 bracelets, 50 brooches and a sword for services rendered.

Anchor			DMC	
Step 1:			Cross-stitch	
1	⊡	◿		White
297	▢		743	Yellow-med.
886	▢	◿	677	Old Gold-vy. lt.
890	▨	◢	729	Old Gold-med.
323	▨	◢	722	Orange Spice-lt.
324	▧	◢	721	Orange Spice-med.
326	■	◢	720	Orange Spice-dk.
24	▢		776	Pink-med.
27	▨		899	Rose-med.
42	■		309	Rose-deep
43	■	◢	815	Garnet-med.
87	■		3607	Plum-lt.
89	▨		917	Plum-med.
158	▨	◿	775	Baby Blue-vy. lt.
159	▨	◿	3325	Baby Blue-lt.
145	■	◢	334	Baby Blue-med.
149	■	◢	311	Navy Blue-med.
185	▢	◿	964	Seagreen-lt.
187	▨		958	Seagreen-dk.
433	■	◿	996	Electric Blue-med.
213	▢	◿	369	Pistachio Green-vy. lt.
209	▨	◿	913	Nile Green-med.
205	■		911	Emerald Green-med.
229	★		909	Emerald Green-vy. dk.
923	■	◢	699	Christmas Green
403	■	◢	310	Black

Step 2: Backstitch

403	⌐	310	Black

Step 3: French Knot

403	●	310	Black

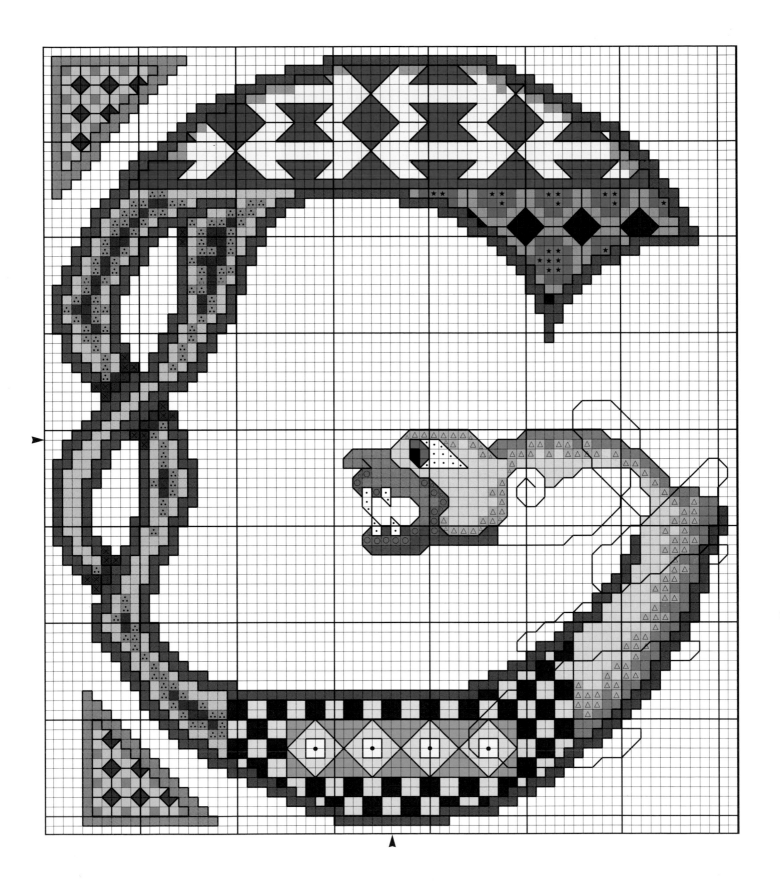

ƕ

Fabric
Aida 11
Aida 14
Aida 18
Hardanger 22

Design Size
6¼" x 6⅞"
4⅞" x 5⅜"
3⅞" x 4⅛"
3⅛" x 3⅜"

Stitch count: 69 x 75

ƕ eroes of Celtic society followed strict rules of martial conduct. Their behavior provided the basis for the medieval code of chivalry.

The Celts were a democratic people. Major decisions were made by consent of assembled freemen. The system functioned around the practice of owning land and the warrior aristocracy.

Law was believed to have been divinely ordained and even a Celtic king adhered to it.

Anchor			DMC	
Step 1:			Cross-stitch	
1	⊡	◿		White
891	▨	◿	676	Old Gold-lt.
890	■	◿	729	Old Gold-med.
301	☐	◿	744	Yellow-pale
297	◉	◿	743	Yellow-med.
303	⊡	◿	742	Tangerine-lt.
323	▨	◿	722	Orange Spice-lt.
324	☒	◿	721	Orange Spice-med.
326	■	◢	720	Orange Spice-dk.
48	☐	◿	818	Baby Pink
24	△	◿	776	Pink-med.
27	▨	◿	899	Rose-med.
46	■	◣	666	Christmas Red-bright
47	▬		304	Christmas Red-med.
43	■	◢	815	Garnet-med.
108	▨	◿	211	Lavender-lt.
104	⊞	◿	210	Lavender-med.
110	■	◣	208	Lavender-vy. dk.
87	■	◿	3607	Plum-lt.
158	☐	◿	775	Baby Blue-vy. lt.
159	▢	◿	3325	Baby Blue-lt.
145	▨	◢	334	Baby Blue-med.
149	■		311	Navy Blue-med.
185	◫	◿	964	Seagreen-lt.
186	▨	◿	959	Seagreen-med.
187	■	◣	958	Seagreen-dk.
255	☐		907	Parrot Green-lt.
256	ⓢ	◿	906	Parrot Green-med.
258	■	◢	904	Parrot Green-vy. dk.
213	☐	◿	369	Pistachio Green-vy. lt.
209	★	◿	913	Nile Green-med.
205	■		911	Emerald Green-med.
229	Ⓝ	◿	909	Emerald Green-vy. dk.

Step 2: Backstitch

403	└┐	310	Black

Step 3: French Knot

403	●	310	Black

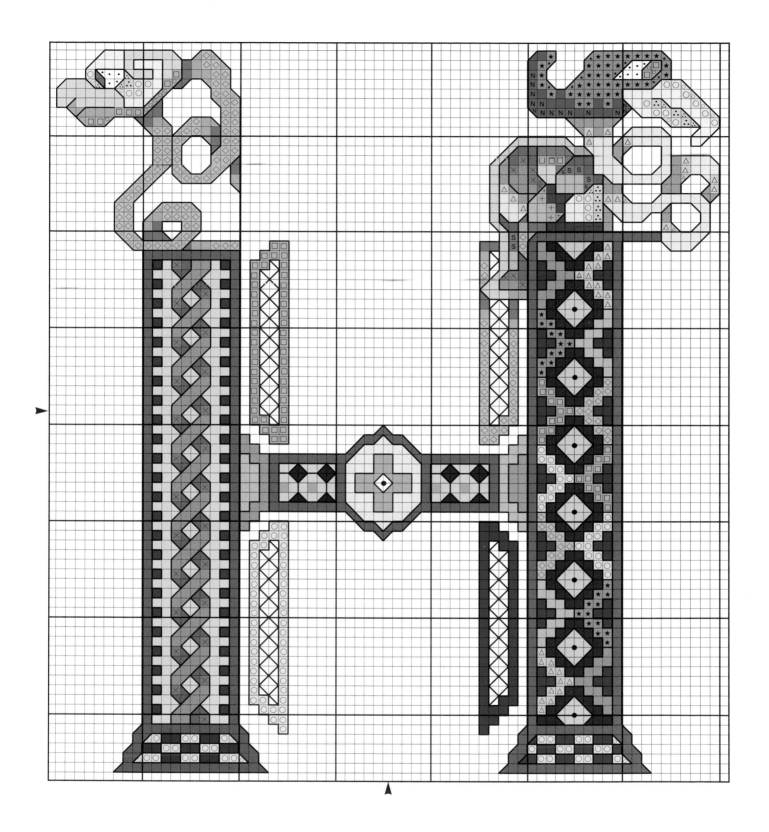

41

l

Fabric	Design Size
Aida 11	6⅜" x 6⅞"
Aida 14	5" x 5⅜"
Aida 18	3⅞" x 4⅛"
Hardanger 22	3¼" x 3⅜"

Stitch count: 70 x 75

Tara is a most sacred place on the island of Ireland. It was designated by the Dannans as the site of the Stone of Destiny, which cries out when the lawful king touches it. It was also the royal site of the palace of Meath, seat of the High Kings of Ireland. It was also the domain of the magical King Eochy.

Anchor			DMC (used for sample)	
Step 1:			Cross-stitch (2 strands)	
1	⊞	◿		White
301	☐	◿	744	Yellow-pale
297	◎		743	Yellow-med.
303	◼	◿	742	Tangerine-lt.
886	⊠	◿	677	Old Gold-vy. lt.
891	◼	◿	676	Old Gold-lt.
890	◮	◿	729	Old Gold-med.
778	⊟	◿	948	Peach-vy. lt.
4146	◼	◿	754	Peach-lt.
6	E	◿	353	Peach
8	◿	◿	761	Salmon-lt.
10	◼		3712	Salmon-med.
11	★	◿	3328	Salmon-dk.
323	◼	◿	722	Orange Spice-lt.
326	◼	◿	720	Orange Spice-dk.
48	☐	◿	818	Baby Pink
35	▨	◿	3705	Melon-dk.
46	◼	◿	666	Christmas Red-bright
47	◼	◿	304	Christmas Red-med.
87	◼	◿	3607	Plum-lt.
98	◼		553	Violet-med.
154	◼	◿	3755	Baby Blue
149	◼	◢	311	Navy Blue-med.
185	◻	◿	964	Seagreen-lt.
206	☐	◿	955	Nile Green-lt.
203	⊡	◿	564	Jade-vy. lt.
208	N	◿	563	Jade-lt.
210	◼	◿	562	Jade-med.

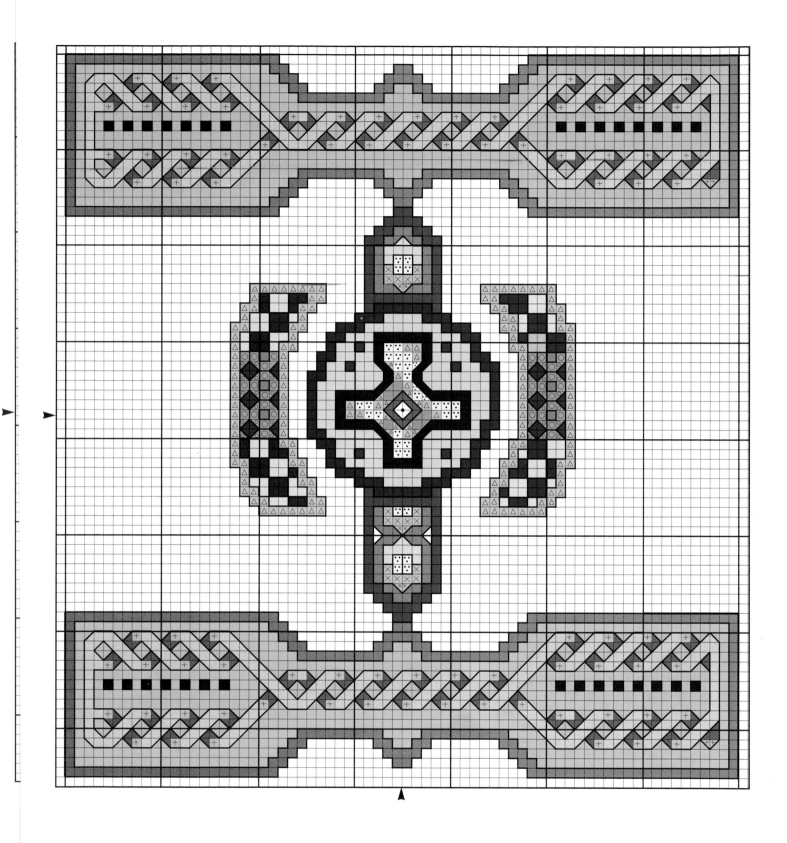

43

k

Fabric	Design Size
Aida 11	6⅜" x 6⅞"
Aida 14	5" x 5½"
Aida 18	3⅞" x 4¼"
Hardanger 22	3⅛" x 3½"

Stitch count: 70 x 76

Upon association with the Celtic people, the Greeks called them "Keltoi," which meant that the people were strangers—different. The Celts were known as one of three most barbarous nations (joining the Persians and the Scythians).

Foreigners who encountered the "Keltoi" described them as a people who kept tribal names, were of notable fierceness, demonstrated egregious behavior, and maintained pronounced social differences.

The Celts are described as a "peacock" people, who loved ornamentation, ritualistic worship, competition in physical contest and intellectual gaming. They were very proud and economically successful.

They were men of presence and women of great beauty, dressing in the brightest colors and finest cloth. They wore their clothing for mood and to express their love of grandure.

Their myths and their lives were fantastic as they embraced the good as well as the bad and they feared only boredom.

Anchor			DMC	
Step 1:			Cross-stitch	
1	⊡	◿		White
886	⊡		677	Old Gold-vy. lt.
891	▣		676	Old Gold-lt.
890	◼		729	Old Gold-med.
297	◻	◿	743	Yellow-med.
303	⊍	◿	742	Tangerine-lt.
323	◼	◿	722	Orange Spice-lt.
24	◻	◿	776	Pink-med.
35	◼		3705	Melon-dk.
46	◼		666	Christmas Red-bright
47	◼		304	Christmas Red-med.
43	◼	◢	815	Garnet-med.
105	◼	◢	209	Lavender-dk.
87	◼	◢	3607	Plum-lt.
89	◼	◢	917	Plum-med.
128	◻	◿	800	Delft-pale
130	◼	◿	799	Delft-med.
185	◻	◿	964	Seagreen-lt.
213	◻		369	Pistachio Green-vy. lt.
209	◉	◢	913	Nile Green-med.
210	◼	◢	562	Jade-med.
246	◼	◢	986	Forest Green-vy. dk.
347	◻	◿	402	Mahogany-vy. lt.
338	◼	◢	3776	Mahogany-lt.
349	⊠	◢	301	Mahogany-med.
351	◼	◢	400	Mahogany-dk.
373	◻	◿	422	Hazel Nut Brown-lt.
375	◼		420	Hazel Nut Brown-dk.
944	◬	◿	869	Hazel Nut Brown-vy. dk.
403	◼		310	Black

Step 2: Backstitch

403	⌐	310	Black

Step 3: French Knot

403	●	310	Black

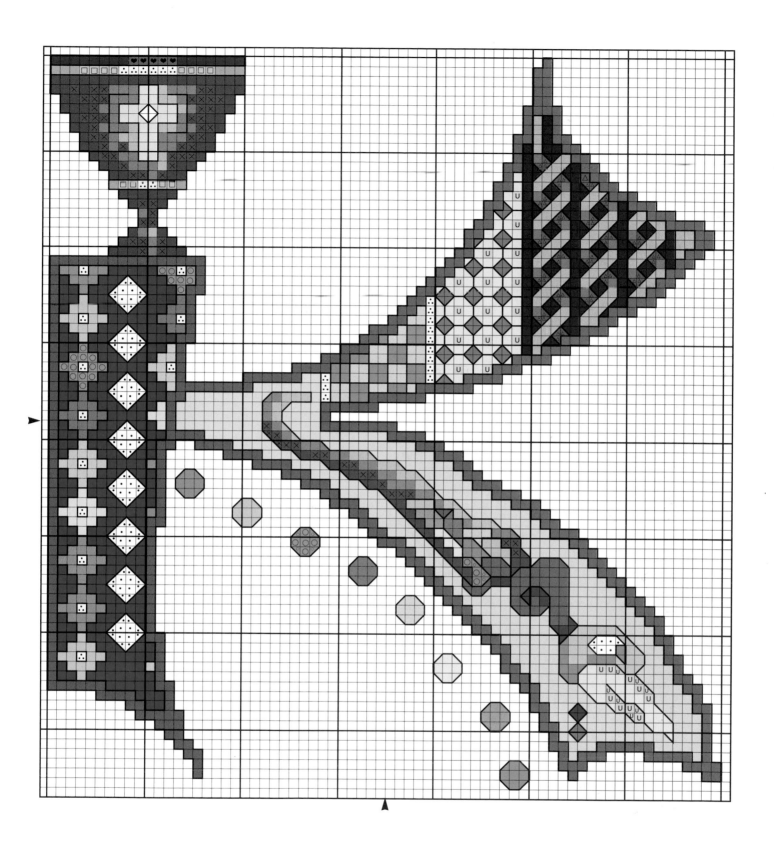

L

Fabric	Design Size
Aida 11	6⅜" x 7¼"
Aida 14	5" x 5¾"
Aida 18	3⅞" x 4½"
Hardanger 22	3⅛" x 3⅝"

Stitch count: 70 x 80

Lugh was the god/king of Dannan, who defeated the horrible one-eyed Formorians. The gods gave him the skies and the fields and all in between, including a rainbow sling, the Milky Way for his necklace, and a boat, the Wave Sweeper, which did not need a helmsman. He had a sword named the "Answerer," and the god of the waves gave him a horse that could ride over land or water.

Lugh rid the land of the Formorians by hurling a stone from his sling deep into the eye of Balor, the Formorian leader, killing him.

Anchor			DMC	
Step 1:		Cross-stitch		
891	□	◿	676	Old Gold-lt.
300	□	◿	745	Yellow-lt. pale
297	▣	◿	743	Yellow-med.
304	▨	◿	741	Tangerine-med.
46	■	◢	666	Christmas Red-bright
48	□	◿	818	Baby Pink
25	◙	◿	3326	Rose-lt.
42	▨	◿	335	Rose
75	⊞	◿	604	Cranberry-lt.
76	▨	◿	603	Cranberry
78	■	◢	601	Cranberry-dk.
105	▨	◿	209	Lavender-dk.
101	■	◢	550	Violet-vy. dk.
85	▨	◿	3609	Plum-ultra lt.
87	▨	◿	3607	Plum-lt.
89	■	◢	917	Plum-med.
158	□	◿	775	Baby Blue-vy. lt.
159	☒	◿	3325	Baby Blue-lt.
145	■	◿	334	Baby Blue-med.
149	■	◢	311	Navy Blue-med.
185	◬	◿	964	Seagreen-lt.
203	▱		564	Jade-vy. lt.
213	E	◿	369	Pistachio Green-vy. lt.
206	□	◿	955	Nile Green-lt.
203	N	◿	954	Nile Green
204	▨	◿	912	Emerald Green-lt.
879	■	◢	890	Pistachio Green-ultra dk.

Step 2:		Backstitch		
403	└─┐		310	Black

48

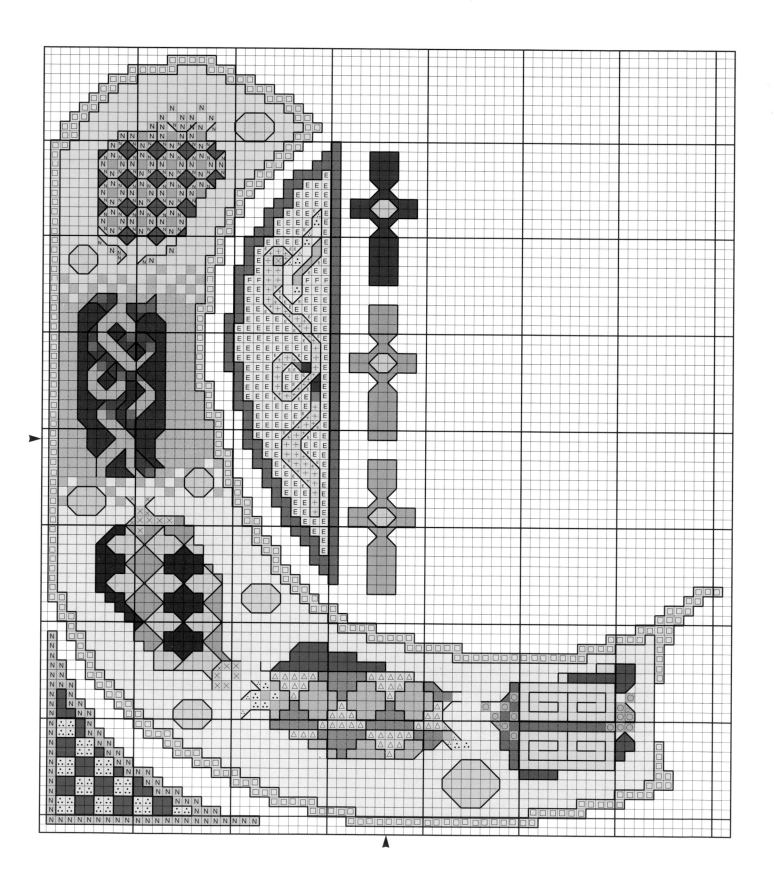

49

ℳ

Fabric	Design Size
Aida 11	6⅜" x 6⅞"
Aida 14	5" x 5⅜"
Aida 18	3⅞" x 4⅛"
Hardanger 22	3⅛" x 3⅜"

Stitch count: 70 x 75

ℳusic was very important in Celtic society. It is believed that the Celts may have assigned certain modes of music to different seasons and times of day. Music is believed to have healing powers and to be able to still the savage.

The Celtic love for song and story practically amounted to addiction. This accounts for much of the power of the Bards, who were the masters of the harp. The basic instruments of the Celts were the harp, the pipe and the crotta, which is similar to a fiddle.

Anchor			DMC	
Step 1:			Cross-stitch	
297	☐		743	Yellow-med.
886	☐	◿	677	Old Gold-vy. lt.
891	◸	◿	676	Old Gold-lt.
890	■		729	Old Gold-med.
24	▨	◿	776	Pink-med.
46	■		666	Christmas Red-bright
43	■	◣	815	Garnet-med.
87	■		3607	Plum-lt.
154	▨	◿	3755	Baby Blue
130	⊠		799	Delft-med.
132	■		797	Royal Blue
185	◎		964	Seagreen-lt.
205	B		911	Emerald Green-med.
203	☐		564	Jade-vy. lt.
210	H		562	Jade-med.
212	■		561	Jade-vy. dk.
373	▨	◿	422	Hazel Nut Brown-lt.
375	■	◢	420	Hazel Nut Brown-dk.
944	■	◢	869	Hazel Nut Brown-vy. dk.

Anchor		DMC	
Step 2:		Backstitch	
403	∟	310	Black

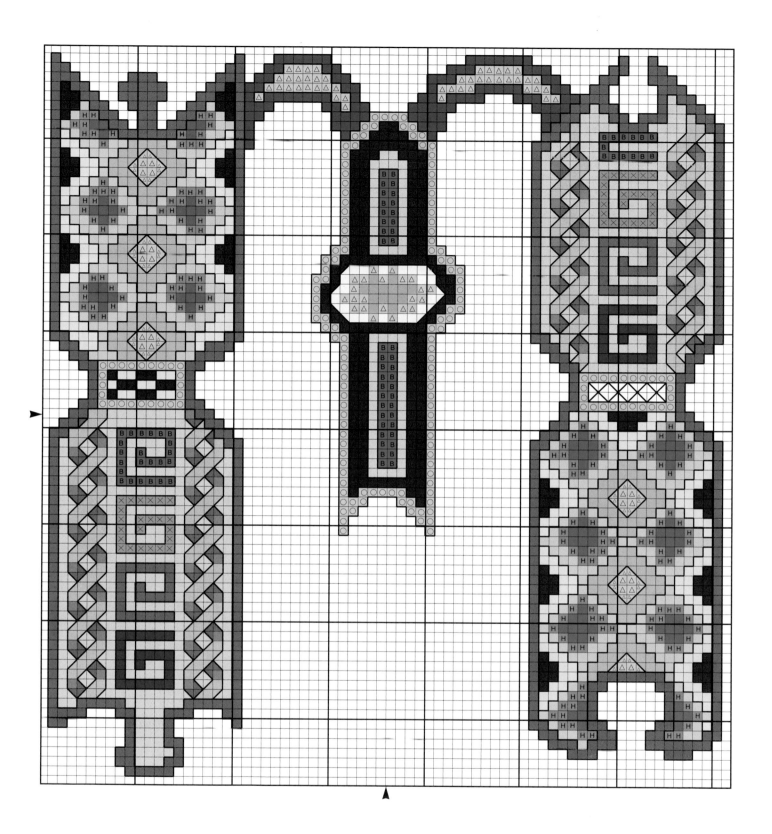

51

N

Fabric

Aida 11
Aida 14
Aida 18
Hardanger 22

Design Size

6⅜" x 6⅞"
5" x 5⅜"
3⅞" x 4⅛"
3⅛" x 3⅜"

Stitch count: 70 x 75

The story is told of Niall, a son of Eochu Muigmedon, King of Ireland, who, while he was out hunting with his four brothers, came upon a hideous woman guarding a well. She was disgusting to look at and everything about her offended the senses. The woman demanded a kiss as the price for the water.

Niall was the only one of the four brothers who kissed her. Upon receiving his kiss, she transformed into a beautiful woman.

Anchor			DMC	
Step 1:			Cross-stitch	
1	⊡	◿		White
891	⊠	◿	676	Old Gold-lt.
301	☐	◿	744	Yellow-pale
297	Ⓤ	◿	743	Yellow-med.
303	▨	◿	742	Tangerine-lt.
323	■	◢	722	Orange Spice-lt.
324	⊞	◢	721	Orange Spice-med.
326	■	◿	720	Orange Spice-dk.
48	☐	◿	818	Baby Pink
25	▨	◢	3326	Rose-lt.
42	■	◢	335	Rose
35	▲	◢	3705	Melon-dk.
46	■	◢	666	Christmas Red-bright
47	▨	◢	304	Christmas Red-med.
87	■		3607	Plum-lt.
104	▨	◿	210	Lavender-med.
105	◎	◿	209	Lavender-dk.
110	■	◢	208	Lavender-vy. dk.
158	☐	◿	775	Baby Blue-vy. lt.
154	⊟	◿	3755	Baby Blue
978	■	◢	322	Navy Blue-vy. lt.
185	▨	◿	964	Seagreen-lt.
186	Ⓢ	◿	959	Seagreen-med.
187	■	◢	958	Seagreen-dk.
203	▨	◿	954	Nile Green
204	▨	◿	912	Emerald Green-lt.
213	☐	◿	369	Pistachio Green-vy. lt.
228	★	◢	910	Emerald Green-dk.
246	■	◢	986	Forest Green-vy. dk.
255	▨	◿	907	Parrot Green-lt.
256	▣		906	Parrot Green-med.
258	■	◿	905	Parrot Green-dk.
403	■	◢	310	Black

Step 2: Backstitch

403	⌐	310	Black

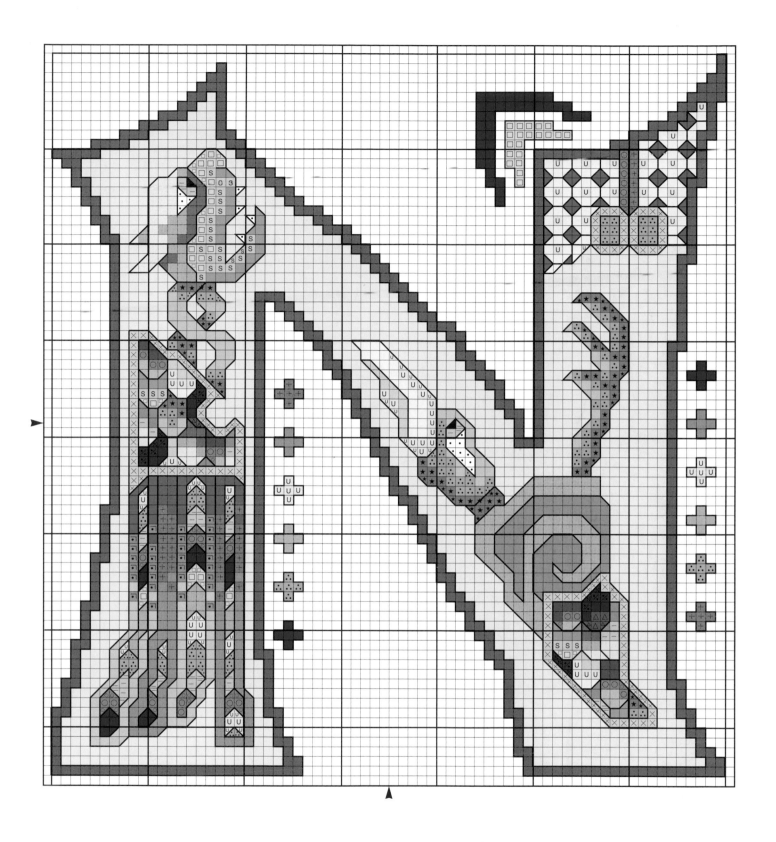

O

Fabric
Aida 11
Aida 14
Aida 18
Hardanger 22

Design Size
6⅜" x 6⅞"
5" x 5½"
3⅞" x 4¼"
3⅛" x 3½"

Stitch count: 70 x 76

At the center of the the swirls in a spiral design is the "omphalos." This is the point where Heaven and earth are joined. The spirals symbolize eternal life. The whorls represent the continuous creation and dissolution of the world. The passages between spirals represent the divisions between life, death and rebirth.

Anchor   **DMC**

Step 1: Cross-stitch

Anchor			DMC	
1	⊡	◿		White
891	▨		676	Old Gold-lt.
301	☐	◿	744	Yellow-pale
297	◎	◿	743	Yellow-med.
303	▨	◿	742	Tangerine-lt.
323	▧	◣	722	Orange Spice-lt.
324	▨	◿	721	Orange Spice-med.
326	▨	◢	720	Orange Spice-dk.
48	☐	◿	818	Baby Pink
24	▣	◿	776	Pink-med.
27	▨	◣	899	Rose-med.
35	☒	◢	3705	Melon-dk.
46	■	◢	666	Christmas Red-bright
47	■	◢	304	Christmas Red-med.
87	▨		3607	Plum-lt.
104	▨	◿	210	Lavender-med.
105	Ⓐ		209	Lavender-dk.
110	▨	◢	208	Lavender-vy. dk.
158	☐	◿	775	Baby Blue-vy. lt.
159	Ⓑ	◿	3325	Baby Blue-lt.
145	▨	◣	334	Baby Blue-med.
147	▨	◢	312	Navy Blue-lt.
213	☐	◿	369	Pistachio Green-vy. lt.
206	▨	◿	955	Nile Green-lt.
203	Ⓦ	◿	564	Jade-vy. lt.
208	Ⓢ	◿	563	Jade-lt.
210	▨	◿	562	Jade-med.
255	▨	◿	907	Parrot Green-lt.
256	Ⓖ	◣	906	Parrot Green-med.
258	▨	◣	905	Parrot Green-dk.
341	■		919	Red Copper
373	☐	◿	422	Hazel Nut Brown-lt.
375	▨		420	Hazel Nut Brown-dk.
944	▨	◿	869	Hazel Nut Brown-vy. dk.
403	■		310	Black

Step 2: Backstitch

403	∟	310	Black

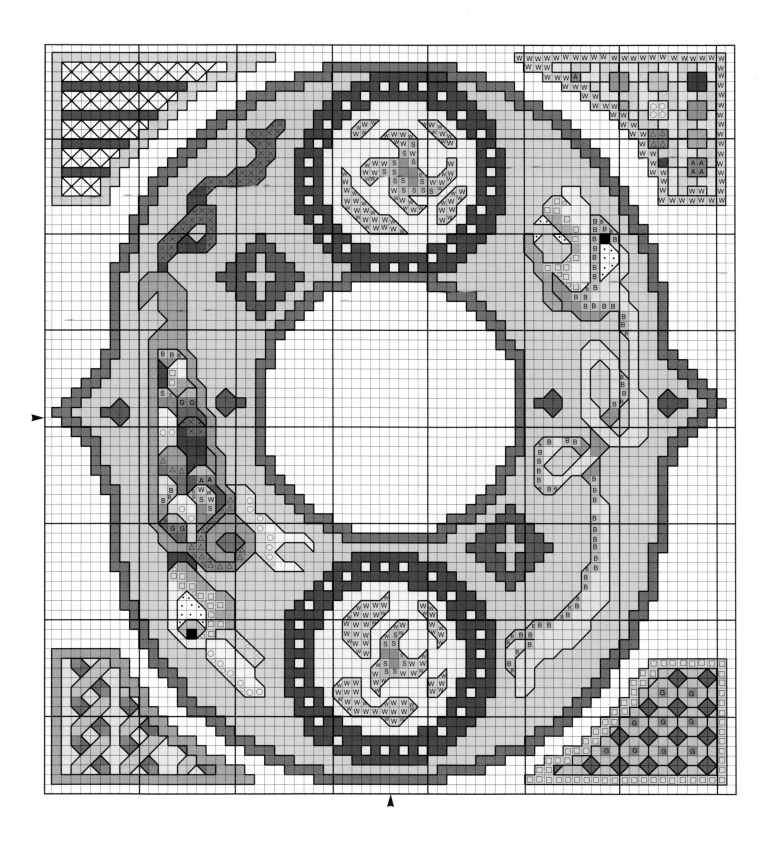

55

p

Fabric

Aida 11
Aida 14
Aida 18
Hardanger 22

Design Size

6⅜" x 6⅞"
5" x 5⅜"
3⅞" x 4⅛"
3¼" x 3⅜"

Stitch count: 70 x 75

Tir na n'Og, which means the "Land of Youth," is the Celtic name for paradise. Upon arriving there, one loses all sense of the passing of time. The otherworld is said to be a place of supreme happiness. It is rich in food and delights of nature. No unpleasantness exists there.

It is very difficult, if not completely impossible, to leave the Land of Youth.

Anchor   **DMC**

Step 1: Cross-stitch

Anchor			DMC	
1	⊡	◿		White
886	☐	◿	677	Old Gold-vy. lt.
890	■		729	Old Gold-med.
301	⊞	◿	744	Yellow-pale
297	△	◿	743	Yellow-med.
303	☐	◿	742	Tangerine-lt.
323	■	◿	722	Orange Spice-lt.
324	⊠	◿	721	Orange Spice-med.
326	■	◸	720	Orange Spice-dk.
48	☐	◿	818	Baby Pink
24	◎		776	Pink-med.
76	■	◢	603	Cranberry
35	■	◢	3705	Melon-dk.
46	■	◢	666	Christmas Red-bright
47	H	◢	304	Christmas Red-med.
43	■	◢	815	Garnet-med.
104	☐	◿	210	Lavender-med.
105	S		209	Lavender-dk.
110	■	◢	208	Lavender-vy. dk.
87	■		3607	Plum-lt.
159	M		3325	Baby Blue-lt.
145	■		334	Baby Blue-med.
185	▣	◿	964	Seagreen-lt.
186	▨		959	Seagreen-med.
187	■	◿	958	Seagreen-dk.
204	K	◿	912	Emerald Green-lt.
246	■	◸	986	Forest Green-vy. dk.
362	☐		437	Tan-lt.
309	■		435	Brown-vy. lt.
360	■		898	Coffee Brown-vy. dk.
403	■		310	Black

Step 2: Backstitch

403	⌐‿	310	Black

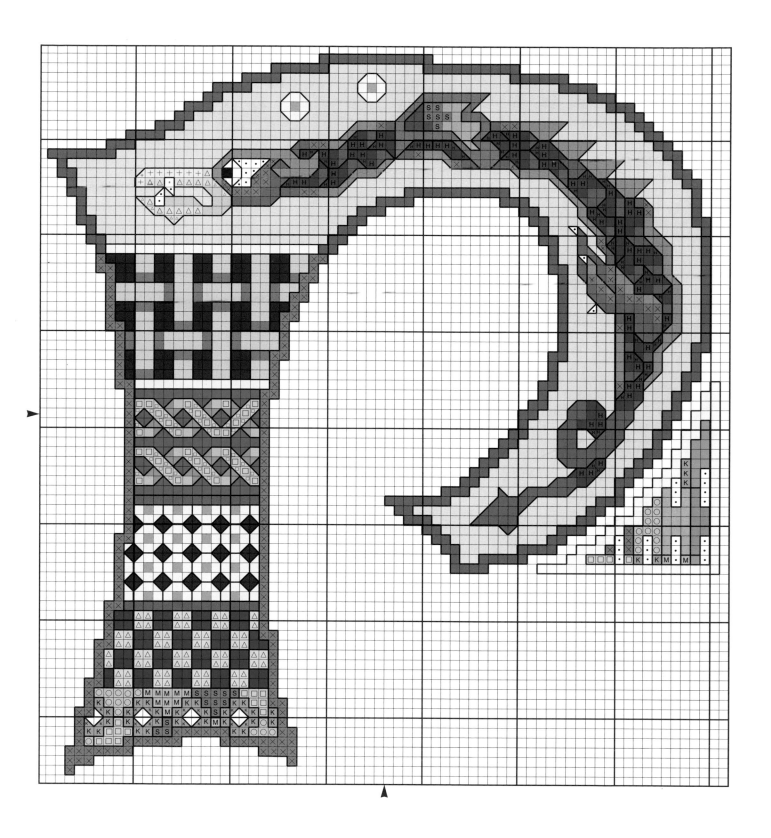

57

q

Fabric
Aida 11
Aida 14
Aida 18
Hardanger 22

Design Size
6¾" x 6¾"
5" x 5"
3⅞" x 3⅞"
3⅛" x 3½"

Stitch count: 70 x 70

The Celtic tribes, at one point, split into two main tribes, the Goidels and the Brythons. Their languages share the same roots. The differences in dialect are often referred to as the Q-Celtic which was Goidelic or of the Gauls. P-Celtic was Brythonic or of the British.

In the P-Celtic dialect, the letters P and B replace the letters C and Q which remain constant in the Q-Celtic dialect. For example, the word "mac," in the Q-Celtic meaning "son," becomes "map" in the P-Celtic.

Anchor			DMC	
Step 1:			Cross-stitch	
886	□	◿	677	Old Gold-vy. lt.
891	◙		676	Old Gold-lt.
890	■		729	Old Gold-med.
297	□	◿	743	Yellow-med.
323	■		722	Orange Spice-lt.
76	■		603	Cranberry
78	■		601	Cranberry-dk.
46	■	◢	666	Christmas Red-bright
47	▲		304	Christmas Red-med.
87	■	◢	3607	Plum-lt.
43	■	◢	815	Garnet-med.
104	□		210	Lavender-med.
105	◙		209	Lavender-dk.
110	■		208	Lavender-vy. dk.
101	■		550	Violet-vy. dk.
158	□	◿	775	Baby Blue-vy. lt.
159	☒		3325	Baby Blue-lt.
145	■		334	Baby Blue-med.
149	■		311	Navy Blue-med.
185	⊞		964	Seagreen-lt.
203	■		954	Nile Green
213	□		369	Pistachio Green-vy. lt.
204	G		912	Emerald Green-lt.
228	■		910	Emerald Green-dk.
246	■		986	Forest Green-vy. dk.

Step 2: Backstitch

403	⌐	310	Black

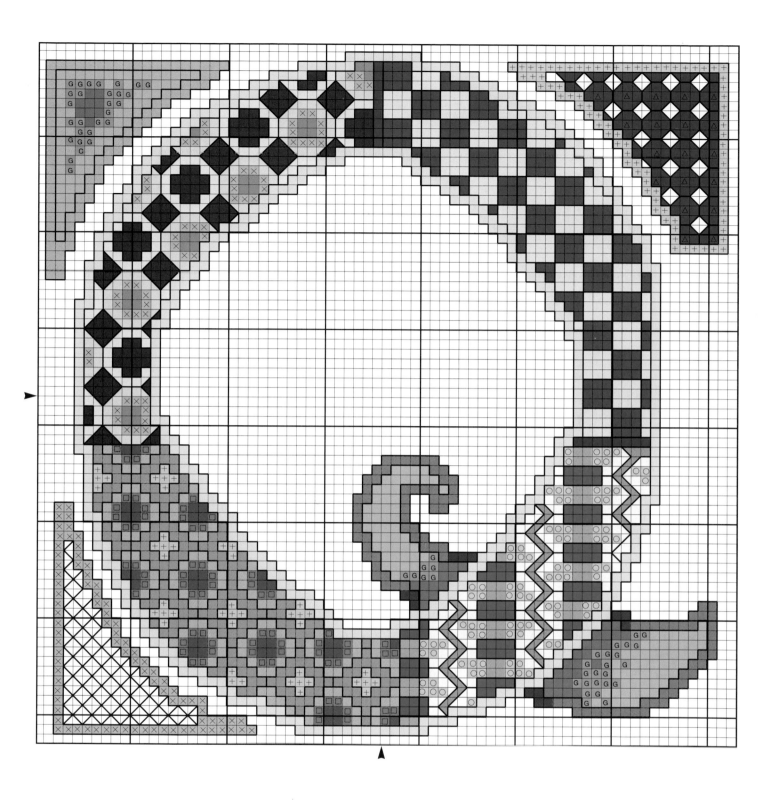

59

R

Fabric

Fabric	Design Size
Aida 11	6¼" x 6⅞"
Aida 14	4⅞" x 5½"
Aida 18	3⅞" x 4¼"
Hardanger 22	3⅛" x 3½"

Stitch count: 69 x 76

Elected from a royal clan, the Rig was the king of a territory. The Rig didn't necessarily have to·be the son of a king. He held administrative and military powers within his kingdom. His most important duties were religious, including maintaining beneficial relations with the gods and goddesses. He also held the right of special judge and arbitrator in cases of royal prerogatives.

Anchor			DMC	
Step 1:		Cross-stitch		
1	·	◿		White
886	K		677	Old Gold-vy. lt.
891	+	◿	676	Old Gold-lt.
890	■	◿	729	Old Gold-med.
301	□	◿	744	Yellow-pale
297	◉	◿	743	Yellow-med.
303	▨	◿	742	Tangerine-lt.
323	■	◿	722	Orange Spice-lt.
324	A	◿	721	Orange Spice-med.
326	■	◿	720	Orange Spice-dk.
48	□	◿	818	Baby Pink
24	◉	◿	776	Pink-med.
27	■	◿	899	Rose-med.
35	W	◢	3705	Melon-dk.
46	■	◢	666	Christmas Red-bright
47	■	◢	304	Christmas Red-med.
87	■	◢	3607	Plum-lt.
104	□	◿	210	Lavender-med.
105	S	◿	209	Lavender-dk.
110	■	◢	208	Lavender-vy. dk.
158	□	◿	775	Baby Blue-vy. lt.
154	B	◿	3755	Baby Blue
978	■	◿	322	Navy Blue-vy. lt.
149	■	◢	311	Navy Blue-med.
185	□	◿	964	Seagreen-lt.
186	⊠	◿	959	Seagreen-med.
187	▨	◿	958	Seagreen-dk.
213	□	◿	369	Pistachio Green-vy. lt.
204	A		912	Emerald Green-lt.
228	★	◿	910	Emerald Green-dk.
255	G	◿	907	Parrot Green-lt.
256	▨	◿	906	Parrot Green-med.
258	■	◢	904	Parrot Green-vy. dk.
203	□	◿	954	Nile Green
246	■	◢	986	Forest Green-vy. dk.
403	■	◢	310	Black

Step 2: Backstitch

403	⌐	310	Black

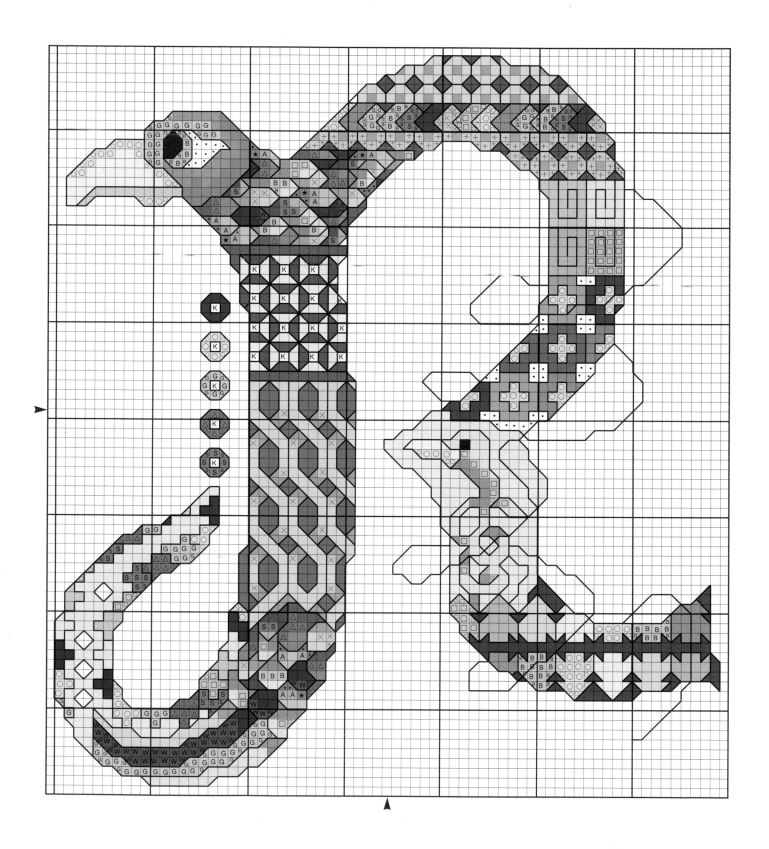

61

S

Fabric	**Design Size**
Aida 11	6⅜" x 6⅝"
Aida 14	5" x 5¼"
Aida 18	3⅞" x 4"
Hardanger 22	3⅛" x 3⅜"

Stitch count: 70 x 73

There are seven created beings of the Celtic world—plants, insects, fish, reptiles, birds, mammals, and man.

Since it was forbidden to copy or portray the works of the Creator, Celtic artists depicted the creatures twisting and intertwining their shapes in knots.

It was believed that the Druids were actually capable of shape-shifting. This ability is reflected in their artwork. Often, an animal is transformed into another upon arrival at the opposite end of the form.

Anchor   **DMC**

Step 1: Cross-stitch

Anchor			DMC	
1	⊡	◿		White
886	⊞	◿	677	Old Gold-vy. lt.
301	☐	◿	744	Yellow-pale
297	◿	◿	743	Yellow-med.
303	☐	◿	742	Tangerine-lt.
24	⊠	◿	776	Pink-med.
50	☐	◿	605	Cranberry-vy. lt.
46	■		666	Christmas Red-bright
47	■		304	Christmas Red-med.
104	☐	◿	210	Lavender-med.
105	☐	◿	209	Lavender-dk.
110	■	◿	208	Lavender-vy. dk.
87	■		3607	Plum-lt.
158	☐	◿	775	Baby Blue-vy. lt.
159	⠒		3325	Baby Blue-lt.
149	■	◢	311	Navy Blue-med.
185	◎	◿	964	Seagreen-lt.
186	★	◿	959	Seagreen-med.
187	■	◿	958	Seagreen-dk.
213	☐		369	Pistachio Green-vy. lt.
203	☐	◿	954	Nile Green
204	H	◿	912	Emerald Green-lt.
228	▼	◿	910	Emerald Green-dk.
246	■	◿	986	Forest Green-vy. dk.
373	☐	◿	422	Hazel Nut Brown-lt.
375	■		420	Hazel Nut Brown-dk.
944	■	◿	869	Hazel Nut Brown-vy. dk.

Step 2: Backstitch

403	└┐	310	Black

Step 3: French Knot

403	●	310	Black

T

Fabric
Aida 11
Aida 14
Aida 18
Hardanger 22

Design Size
6⅜" x 6⅞"
5" x 5⅜"
3⅞" x 4⅛"
3⅛" x 3⅜"

Stitch count: 70 x 75

The basic unit of Celtic society was the "tuath," which meant "people" or "tribe." The word "tuath" eventually was used in reference to the territory which the people occupied. The head of the tuath was the Rig. The social unit was the clan, or "fine." The clan held all land in common so that it could not be disposed of by any one individual.

Anchor			DMC	
Step 1:	Cross-stitch			
886	◎	◿	677	Old Gold-vy. lt.
303	☐		742	Tangerine-lt.
323	M		722	Orange Spice-lt.
337	☐	◿	3778	Terra Cotta
5968	▨		355	Terra Cotta-dk.
24	☐		776	Pink-med.
46	■	◿	666	Christmas Red-bright
85	☐	◿	3609	Plum-ultra lt.
87	■	◿	3607	Plum-lt.
89	■	◢	917	Plum-med.
105	■	◿	209	Lavender-dk.
154	☐		3755	Baby Blue
213	☐		369	Pistachio Green-vy. lt.
203	☒		564	Jade-vy. lt.
212	■	◢	561	Jade-vy. dk.
203	☐	◿	954	Nile Green
204	◮		912	Emerald Green-lt.
228	■		910	Emerald Green-dk.
256	■		906	Parrot Green-med.
942	☐	◿	738	Tan-vy. lt.
363	⊡		436	Tan
370	■	◢	434	Brown-lt.
360	■	◢	898	Coffee Brown-vy. dk.

Step 2:	Backstitch			
403	└─┐		310	Black

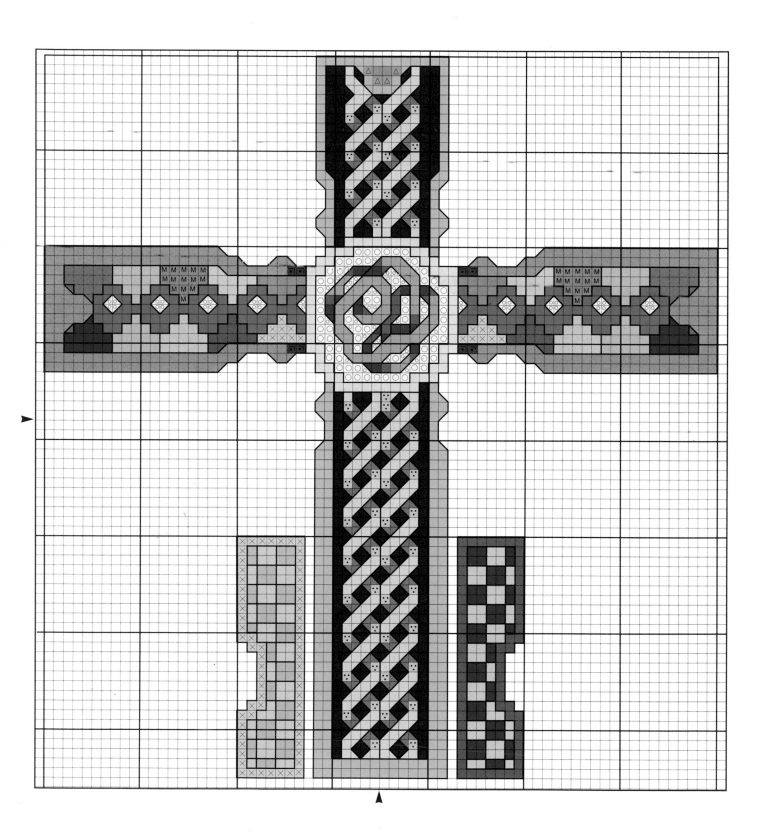

U

Fabric
Aida 11
Aida 14
Aida 18
Hardanger 22

Design Size
6⅜" x 6⅞"
5" x 5½"
3⅞" x 4¼"
3⅛" x 3½"

Stitch count: 70 x 76

Trees were regarded with reverence. They were partakers of mortality and immortality alike. Their roots lay in the underworld while their trunks resided in the earth world and their branches reached to the skies.

Edges of forests, fields, and flowing rivers were seen as gateways between the material and supernatural worlds. They were often designated as places of worship and thought to be blessed with healing powers.

Anchor			DMC	
Step 1:		Cross-stitch		
1	⊡	◿		White
301	☐	◿	744	Yellow-pale
297	⊡	◿	743	Yellow-med.
303	☐		742	Tangerine-lt.
48	☐	◿	818	Baby Pink
24	☐	◿	776	Pink-med.
25	☐		3326	Rose-lt.
27	▣	◿	899	Rose-med.
42	▩		335	Rose
35	▣	◢	3705	Melon-dk.
46	■		666	Christmas Red-bright
47	◩	◢	304	Christmas Red-med.
43	■		815	Garnet-med.
87	▩		3607	Plum-lt.
105	▩	◿	209	Lavender-dk.
101	■	◣	550	Violet-vy. dk.
158	☐	◿	775	Baby Blue-vy. lt.
128	Ⓢ	◿	800	Delft-pale
129	▩	◿	809	Delft
130	◎	◿	799	Delft-med.
131	■	◢	798	Delft-dk.
132	■	◣	797	Royal Blue
185	☐	◿	964	Seagreen-lt.
213	☐	◿	369	Pistachio Green-vy. lt.
203	☐	◿	564	Jade-vy. lt.
208	⊎	◿	563	Jade-lt.
210	▩	◢	562	Jade-med.
204	⊠	◢	912	Emerald Green-lt.
942	☐	◿	738	Tan-vy. lt.
363	☐	◿	436	Tan
370	▩	◢	434	Brown-lt.
403	■	◢	310	Black
Step 2:		Backstitch		
403	└┐		310	Black

66

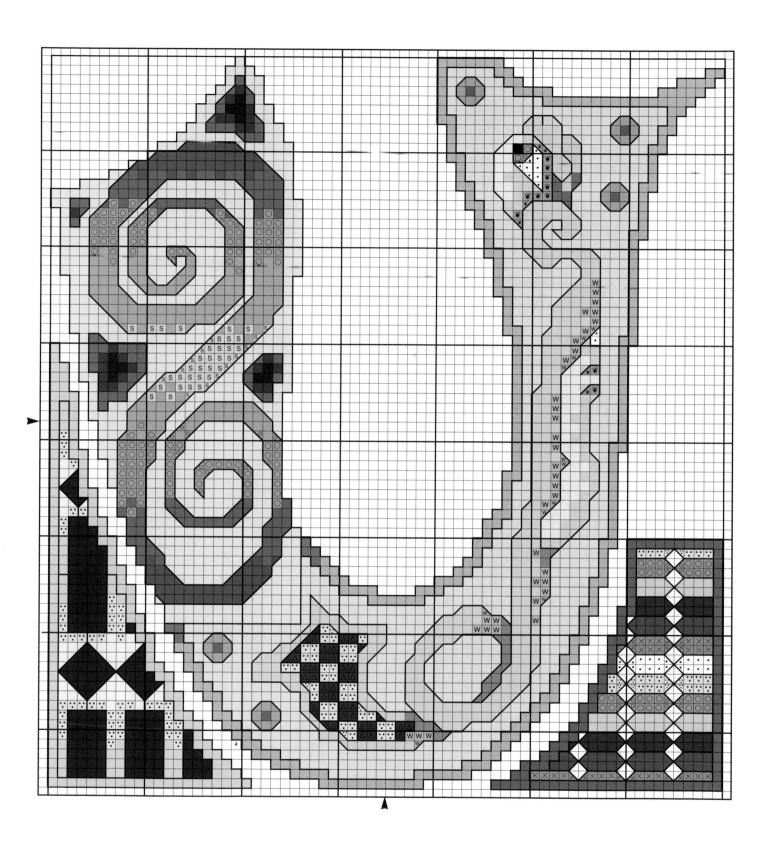

V

Fabric
Aida 11
Aida 14
Aida 18
Hardanger 22

Design Size
6⅜" x 7"
5" x 5½"
3⅞" x 4¼"
3⅛" x 3½"

Stitch count: 70 x 77

Celtic warrior often gained victory in battle by using his frightful appearance as an effective weapon. He would go into combat naked, with his hair matted with lime, and war paint on his face and body. (In Ulster it was called "battle fury.") The enemy would lose heart at the sight of such a demonic guise.

Prisoners were rarely taken. The fate of the defeated was either slavery or beheading. The Celts believed the head to be very powerful. To leave the head of a dead warrior at the battle site was extremely degrading to its power. The head was believed to be the sacred and human center and the soul's resting place. They believed the potency of the head remained after death and its power could be used by its possessor to guard him from evil.

Anchor			DMC	
Step 1:		Cross-stitch		
886	⊞	◿	677	Old Gold-vy. lt.
301	☐	◿	744	Yellow-pale
297	⊡	◿	743	Yellow-med.
303	☐	◿	742	Tangerine-lt.
323	■		722	Orange Spice-lt.
48	☐	◿	818	Baby Pink
24	E		776	Pink-med.
27	■	◢	899	Rose-med.
35	■	◢	3705	Melon-dk.
46	■	◢	666	Christmas Red-bright
47	W	◢	304	Christmas Red-med.
43	■		815	Garnet-med.
104	■	◢	210	Lavender-med.
105	N	◢	209	Lavender-dk.
110	■	◢	208	Lavender-vy. dk.
87	■		3607	Plum-lt.
158	⊠	◿	775	Baby Blue-vy. lt.
159	☐		3325	Baby Blue-lt.
145	■	◢	334	Baby Blue-med.
185	☐	◿	964	Seagreen-lt.
186	S	◿	959	Seagreen-med.
187	■	◢	958	Seagreen-dk.
213	☐	◿	369	Pistachio Green-vy. lt.
255	☐	◿	907	Parrot Green-lt.
256	U	◢	906	Parrot Green-med.
258	♥	◢	904	Parrot Green-vy. dk.
246	■	◢	986	Forest Green-vy. dk.
373	☐	◿	422	Hazel Nut Brown-lt.
375	■	◢	420	Hazel Nut Brown-dk.
944	■	◢	869	Hazel Nut Brown-vy. dk.

Step 2: Backstitch

403	└┐	310	Black

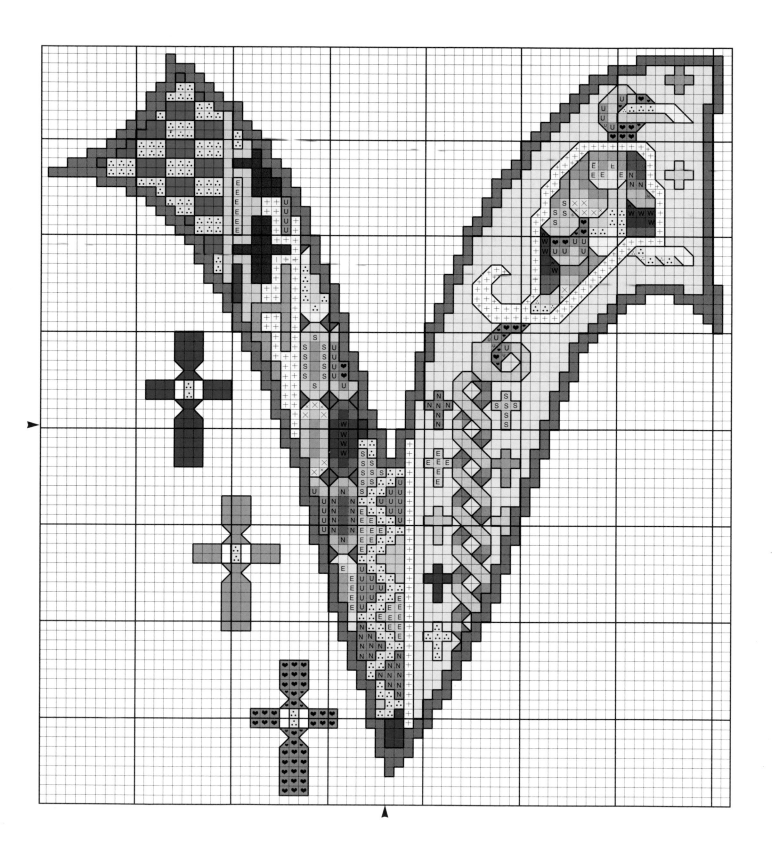

69

w

Fabric   **Design Size**
Aida 11   6⅜" x 6⅞"
Aida 14   5" x 5½"
Aida 18   3⅞" x 4¼"
Hardanger 22   3⅛" x 3½"

Stitch count: 70 x 76

ßoly wells and pools have been discovered that are believed to have been sacred sources of power with therapeutic properties.

The largest amount of Celtic artifacts have been found in lakes and rivers. It is assumed that these may have been offerings to pagan gods.

Anchor			DMC	
Step 1:			Cross-stitch	
886	⊡	◿	677	Old Gold-vy. lt.
891	w	◿	676	Old Gold-lt.
890	◼		729	Old Gold-med.
297	☐	◿	743	Yellow-med.
323	◼	◿	722	Orange Spice-lt.
24	◼	◿	776	Pink-med.
25	◎	◿	3326	Rose-lt.
77	◼	◢	602	Cranberry-med.
46	◼	◢	666	Christmas Red-bright
47	◼		304	Christmas Red-med.
105	◼	◿	209	Lavender-dk.
145	◼	◿	334	Baby Blue-med.
149	◼		311	Navy Blue-med.
185	◼	◿	964	Seagreen-lt.
213	△		369	Pistachio Green-vy. lt.
204	◼	◿	912	Emerald Green-lt.
246	◼		986	Forest Green-vy. dk.
373	◼	◿	422	Hazel Nut Brown-lt.
944	◼	◿	869	Hazel Nut Brown-vy. dk.

Step 2:		Backstitch	
403	└─┐	310	Black

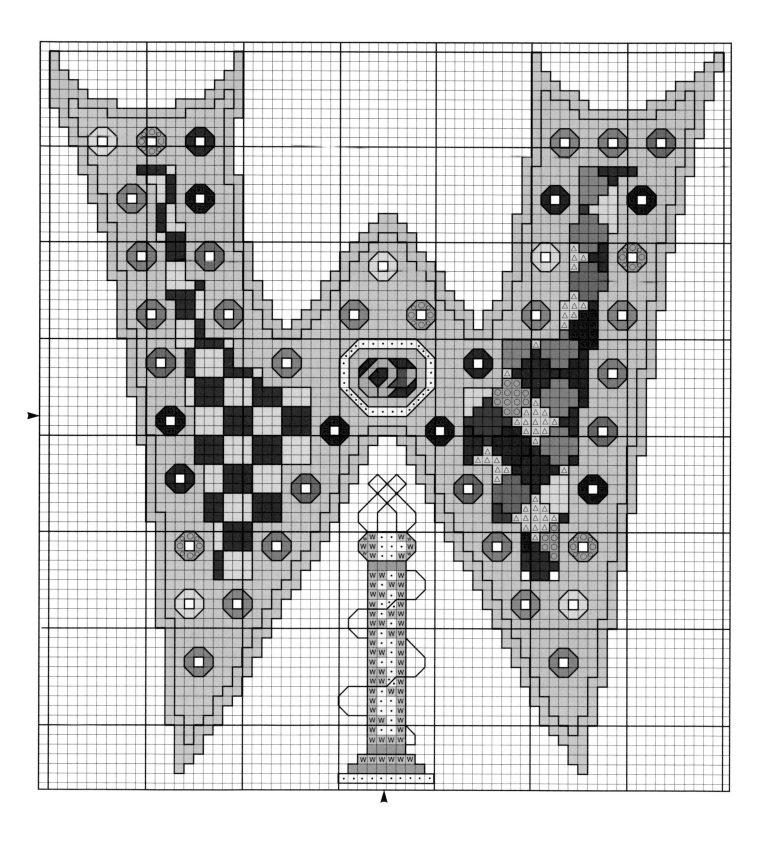

X

Fabric	Design Size
Aida 11	6⅜" x 6¾"
Aida 14	5" x 5¼"
Aida 18	3⅞" x 4⅛"
Hardanger 22	3⅛" x 3⅜"

Stitch count: 70 x 74

Serpents were creatures of the underworld. They were considered magical because they had knowledge of the life cycle concerning the mysteries of death, life and rebirth.

Anchor			DMC	
Step 1:			Cross-stitch	
1	⊡	◿		White
886	☐	◿	677	Old Gold-vy. lt.
891	N	◿	676	Old Gold-lt.
890	◼	◿	729	Old Gold-med.
301	⊞	◿	744	Yellow-pale
297	☐	◿	743	Yellow-med.
303	★	◿	742	Tangerine-lt.
323	◼	◿	722	Orange Spice-lt.
324	◻	◿	721	Orange Spice-med.
326	◼	◢	720	Orange Spice-dk.
25	◻	◿	3326	Rose-lt.
77	◼	◢	602	Cranberry-med.
46	◼	◢	666	Christmas Red-bright
43	◼	◢	815	Garnet-med.
105	◼	◿	209	Lavender-dk.
87	◼		3607	Plum-lt.
89	♥		917	Plum-med.
158	☐	◿	775	Baby Blue-vy. lt.
159	E	◿	3325	Baby Blue-lt.
145	◼	◢	334	Baby Blue-med.
186	◻	◿	959	Seagreen-med.
213	☐	◿	369	Pistachio Green-vy. lt.
203	◻	◿	954	Nile Green
204	M	◿	912	Emerald Green-lt.
228	◼	◢	910	Emerald Green-dk.
373	☐	◿	422	Hazel Nut Brown-lt.
375	◼		420	Hazel Nut Brown-dk.
944	◼	◢	869	Hazel Nut Brown-vy. dk.

Step 2:			Backstitch	
403	└┐		310	Black

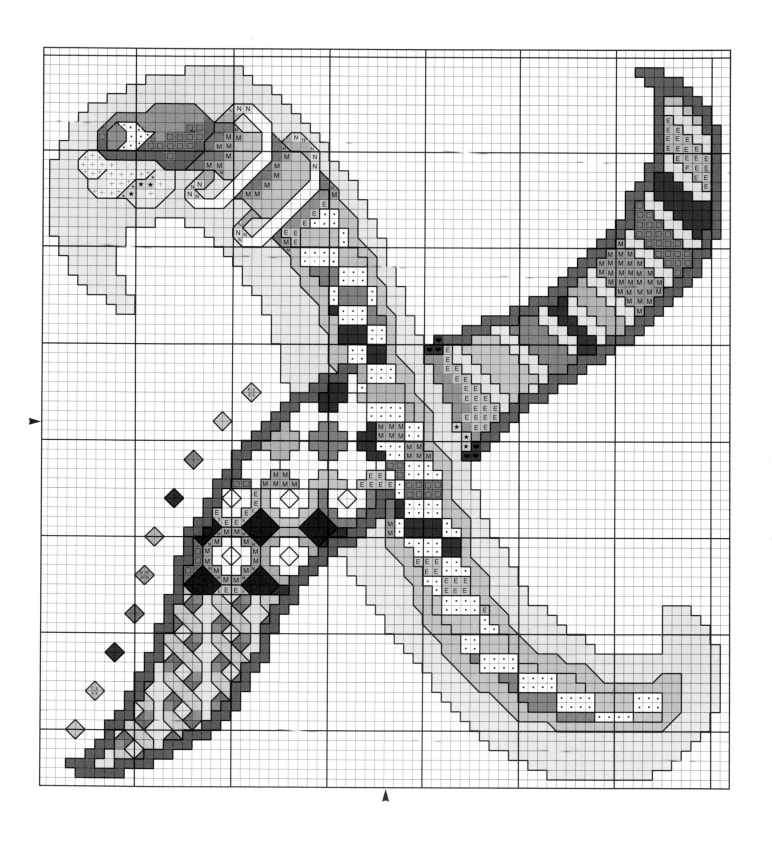

Y

Fabric	Design Size
Aida 11	6⅜" x 6⅞"
Aida 14	5" x 5⅜"
Aida 18	3⅞" x 4⅛"
Hardanger 22	3⅛" x 3⅜"

Stitch count: 70 x 75

pagan tradition and Christianity found common ground in the planting of the yew tree. The yew was regarded as the death tree and was planted around graveyards long after other pagan traditions subsided.

Anchor			DMC	

Step 1: Cross-stitch

Anchor			DMC	
886	□	◿	677	Old Gold-vy. lt.
891	▨	◿	676	Old Gold-lt.
890	E	◿	729	Old Gold-med.
297	⊡		743	Yellow-med.
24	▨	◿	776	Pink-med.
25	△		3326	Rose-lt.
75	Z	◿	604	Cranberry-lt.
76	▨	◢	603	Cranberry
78	■	◢	601	Cranberry-dk.
35	▨		3705	Melon-dk.
46	■		666	Christmas Red-bright
47	N		304	Christmas Red-med.
43	■	◢	815	Garnet-med.
86	U		3608	Plum-vy. lt.
87	▨		3607	Plum-lt.
105	▨		209	Lavender-dk.
159	▨	◿	3325	Baby Blue-lt.
149	■	◢	311	Navy Blue-med.
213	□	◿	369	Pistachio Green-vy. lt.
206	▨	◿	564	Jade-vy. lt.
203	◎		954	Nile Green
204	▨		912	Emerald Green-lt.
228	▨		910	Emerald Green-dk.
187	▨		992	Aquamarine

Step 2: Backstitch

Anchor		DMC	
403	└─┐	310	Black

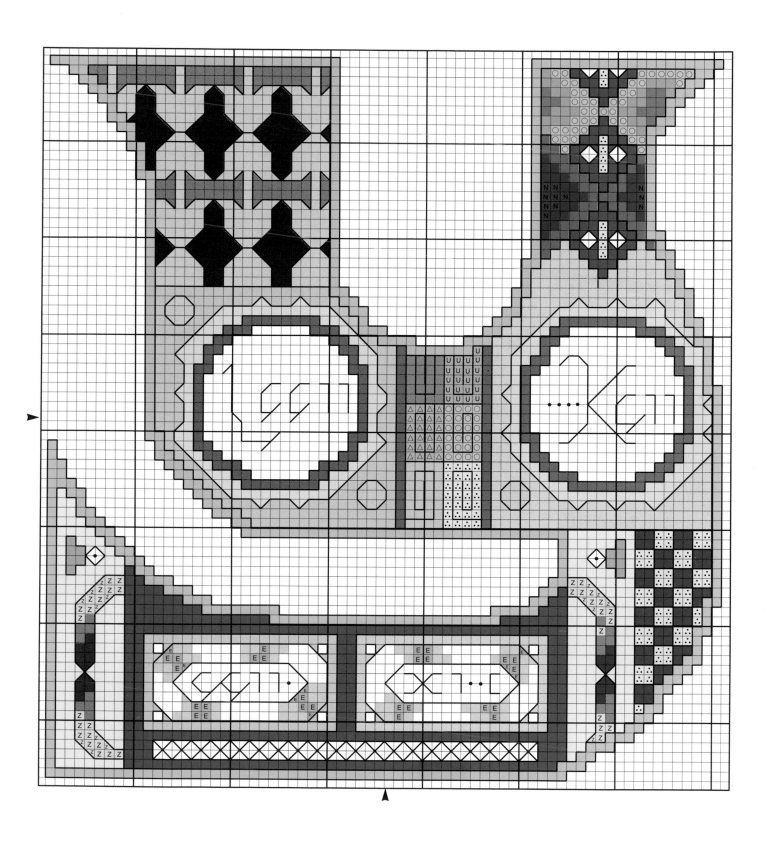

75

Z

Fabric	Design Size
Aida 11	6¼" x 6⅞"
Aida 14	4⅞" x 5⅜"
Aida 18	3⅞" x 4⅛"
Hardanger 22	3⅛" x 3⅜"

Stitch count: 69 x 75

Ornaments depicting zoomorphic creatures that change shape and form are evidence that nothing is as it first appears. In the Book of Kells, three of the four evangelists are depicted as beasts. Matthew is drawn as a man, Mark as a lion, Luke as a calf and John as an eagle.

Anchor   **DMC**

Step 1: Cross-stitch

Anchor			DMC	
1	·	◹		White
891	▫	◹	676	Old Gold-lt.
890	E	◹	729	Old Gold-med.
301	▫	◹	744	Yellow-pale
297	★	◹	743	Yellow-med.
303	▫	◹	742	Tangerine-lt.
323	▫	◹	722	Orange Spice-lt.
324	▲	◹	721	Orange Spice-med.
326	▪	◹	720	Orange Spice-dk.
27	▫		899	Rose-med.
35	S	◹	3705	Melon-dk.
46	▪	◹	666	Christmas Red-bright
47	M	◹	304	Christmas Red-med.
43	▪	◢	815	Garnet-med.
108	▫	◹	211	Lavender-lt.
104	◉	◹	210	Lavender-med.
105	♥	◹	209	Lavender-dk.
110	▪	◢	208	Lavender-vy. dk.
87	▪		3607	Plum-lt.
89	▓	◹	917	Plum-med.
158	▫	◹	775	Baby Blue-vy. lt.
159	G	◹	3325	Baby Blue-lt.
145	▪	◹	334	Baby Blue-med.
185	▣	◹	964	Seagreen-lt.
186	▫	◹	959	Seagreen-med.
187	▪	◹	958	Seagreen-dk.
213	▫	◹	369	Pistachio Green-vy. lt.
203	▫	◹	954	Nile Green
204	H	◹	912	Emerald Green-lt.
228	▪	◹	910	Emerald Green-dk.
373	▫	◹	422	Hazel Nut Brown-lt.
375	▪		420	Hazel Nut Brown-dk.
944	▪	◢	869	Hazel Nut Brown-vy. dk.
403	▪	◢	310	Black

Step 2: Backstitch

403	└─┐	310	Black

Step 3: French Knot

403	●	310	Black

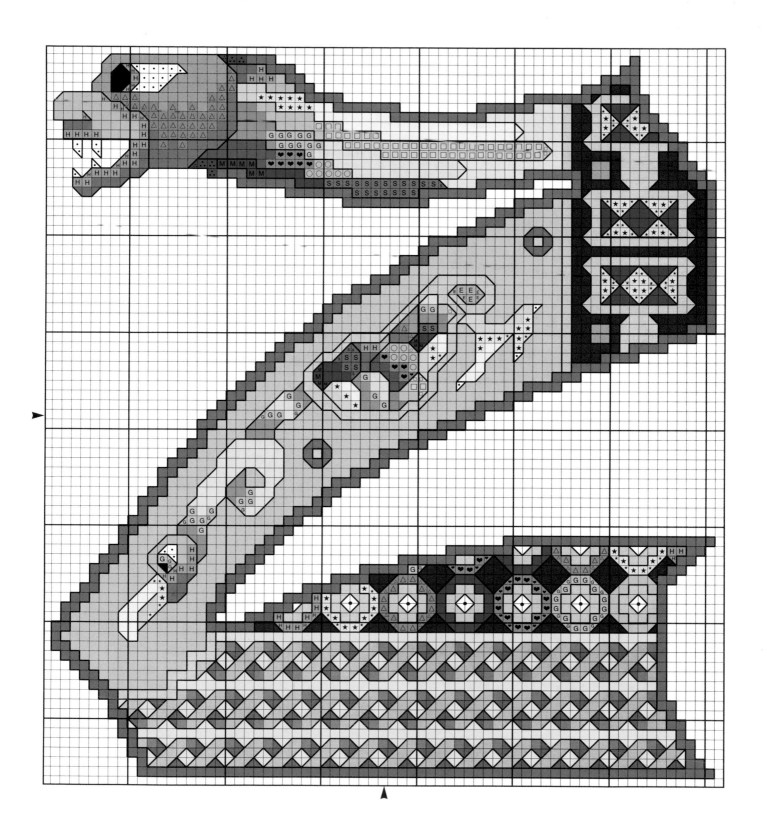

MANANNAN MAC LIR

Stitched on cream Belfast linen 32 over 2
threads, the finished design size is 8¾" x 10".
The fabric was cut 15" x 16".

Fabric	Design Size
Aida 11	12¾" x 14⅝"
Aida 14	10" x 11½"
Aida 18	7¾" x 9"
Hardanger 22	6⅜" x 7⅞"

God of the waves, Manannan mac Lir
was also called Barinthus. He dealt
kindly with such notable heroes as
Cuchullain. Manannan mac Lir is said to have
been the basis for Shakespeare's King Leer.

Stitch count: 140 x 161

Anchor			DMC (used for sample)	

Step 1: Cross-stitch (2 strands)

Anchor			DMC	Color
1	⊞	◢		White
301	☐	◢	744	Yellow-pale
297	◉		743	Yellow-med.
303	☐	◢	742	Tangerine-lt.
886	⊠	◢	677	Old Gold-vy. lt.
891	☐	◢	676	Old Gold-lt.
890	◮	◢	729	Old Gold-med.
778	⊟	◢	948	Peach-vy. lt.
4146	☐	◢	754	Peach-lt.
6	E	◢	353	Peach
8	◩	◢	761	Salmon-lt.
10	■		3712	Salmon-med.
11	★	◢	3328	Salmon-dk.
323	■	◢	722	Orange Spice-lt.
326	■	◢	720	Orange Spice-dk.
48	☐	◢	818	Baby Pink
35	▨	◢	3705	Melon-dk.
46	■	◢	666	Christmas Red-bright
47	■	◢	304	Christmas Red-med.
87	■	◢	3607	Plum-lt.
98	■		553	Violet-med.
154	☐	◢	3755	Baby Blue
149	■	◢	311	Navy Blue-med.
185	☐	◢	964	Seagreen-lt.
206	☐	◢	955	Nile Green-lt.
203	⊡	◢	564	Jade-vy. lt.
208	N	◢	563	Jade-lt.
210	■	◢	562	Jade-med.
255	☐	◢	907	Parrot Green-lt.
256	▲	◢	906	Parrot Green-med:
258	■	◢	904	Parrot Green-vy. dk.
842	☐	◢	3013	Khaki Green-lt.
844	U		3012	Khaki Green-med.
845	■	◢	3011	Khaki Green-dk.
387	S	◢	822	Beige Gray-lt.
830	M	◢	644	Beige Gray-med.
362	☐	◢	437	Tan-lt.
309	■	◢	435	Brown-vy. lt.
360	■	◢	898	Coffee Brown-vy. dk.
397	J	◢	762	Pearl Gray-vy. lt.
399	■	◢	318	Steel Gray-lt.

Step 2: Backstitch (1 strand)

403	⌐	310	Black

Step 3: French Knot (1 strand)

403	●	310	Black

Manannan mac Lir   Bottom Left

Anchor   DMC (used for sample)

Step 1: Cross-stitch (2 strands)

1	⊞ ◸		White	
301	☐ ◸	744	Yellow-pale	
297	◉	743	Yellow-med.	
303	☐ ◸	742	Tangerine-lt.	
886	⊠ ◸	677	Old Gold-vy. lt.	
891	☐ ◸	676	Old Gold-lt.	
890	▲ ◸	729	Old Gold-med.	
778	⊟ ◸	948	Peach-vy. lt.	
4146	☐ ◸	754	Peach-lt.	
6	E ◸	353	Peach	
8	⊠ ◸	761	Salmon-lt.	
10	■	3712	Salmon-med.	

11	★ ◸	3328	Salmon-dk.	
323	■ ◸	722	Orange Spice-lt.	
326	■ ◸	720	Orange Spice-dk.	
48	☐ ◸	818	Baby Pink	
35	■ ◸	3705	Melon-dk.	
46	■ ◸	666	Christmas Red-bright	
47	■ ◸	304	Christmas Red-med.	
87	■ ◸	3607	Plum-lt.	
98	■	553	Violet-med.	
154	☐ ◸	3755	Baby Blue	
149	■ ◸	311	Navy Blue-med.	
185	☐ ◸	964	Seagreen-lt.	

Manannan mac Lir   Bottom Right

206	☐	◿	955	Nile Green-lt.		
203	⊡	◿	564	Jade-vy. lt.		
208	Ⓝ	◿	563	Jade-lt.		
210	☐	◿	562	Jade-med.		
255	☐	◿	907	Parrot Green-lt.		
256	▲	◿	906	Parrot Green-med.		
258	☐	◿	904	Parrot Green-vy. dk.		
842	☐	◿	3013	Khaki Green-lt.		
844	Ⓤ		3012	Khaki Green-med.		
845	☐	◿	3011	Khaki Green-dk.		
387	Ⓢ	◿	822	Beige Gray-lt.		
830	Ⓜ	◿	644	Beige Gray-med.		

362	☐	◿	437	Tan-lt.
309	☐	◢	435	Brown-vy. lt.
360	■	◢	898	Coffee Brown-vy. dk.
397	Ⓙ	◿	762	Pearl Gray-vy. lt.
399	☐	◢	318	Steel Gray-lt.

Step 2: Backstitch (1 strand)

403	└┐	310	Black

Step 3: French Knot (1 strand)

403	●	310	Black

CARPET PAGE

Stitched on cream Belfast linen 32 over 2
threads, the finished design size is 7" x 8¾".
The fabric was cut 13" x 15".

Fabric	Design Size
Aida 11	10⅛" x 12⅝"
Aida 14	7⅞" x 9⅞"
Aida 18	6⅛" x 7¾"
Hardanger 22	5" x 6⅜"

Stitch count: 111 x 139

The carpet page of an illuminated manuscript was an introductory page to the text that followed. Carpet pages were richly ornamented with elaborate Celtic spirals and interlaces. They also featured floral, animal, human and fantastic elements.

Anchor			DMC	(used for sample)

Step 1: Cross-stitch (2 strands)

Anchor			DMC	Color
1	⊡	◿		White
386	◎	◿	746	Off White
301	☐	◿	744	Yellow-pale
297	⊡	◿	743	Yellow-med.
303	▨	◿	742	Tangerine-lt.
886	☐	◿	677	Old Gold-vy. lt.
891	▨	◿	676	Old Gold-lt.
890	■	◿	729	Old Gold-med.
323	▨	◢	722	Orange Spice-lt.
35	■	◢	3705	Melon-dk.
46	■	◢	666	Christmas Red-bright
47	■	◢	304	Christmas Red-med.
24	▨	◿	776	Pink-med.
87	■		3607	Plum-lt.
95	▨	◢	554	Violet-lt.
98	▨	◢	553	Violet-med.
101	■	◢	550	Violet-vy. dk.
158	☐	◿	775	Baby Blue-vy. lt.
154	☒	◿	3755	Baby Blue
978	■	◢	322	Navy Blue-vy. lt.
149	■	◢	311	Navy Blue-med.
206	▨	◿	955	Nile Green-lt.
209	N	◢	913	Nile Green-med.
205	■	◢	911	Emerald Green-med.
203	+	◿	564	Jade-vy. lt.
208	▨	◿	563	Jade-lt.
210	▨	◢	562	Jade-med.
387	U	◿	822	Beige Gray-lt.
830	S	◿	644	Beige Gray-med.
362	▨	◿	437	Tan-lt.
309	■	◢	435	Brown-vy. lt.
403	■	◢	310	Black

Step 2: Backstitch (1 strand)

43	∟	815	Garnet-med.
403	∟	310	Black

Step 3: French Knot (1 strand)

403	●	310	Black

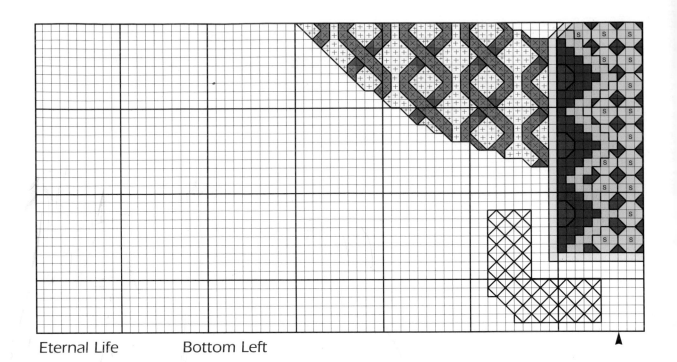

Eternal Life   Bottom Left

Anchor   DMC (used for sample)

Step 1: Cross-stitch (2 strands)

886			677	Old Gold-vy. lt.
289			307	Lemon
297			743	Yellow-med.
303			742	Tangerine-lt.
330			947	Burnt Orange
333			900	Burnt Orange-dk.
46			666	Christmas Red-bright

25			3326	Rose-lt.
42			309	Rose-deep
44			814	Garnet-dk.
108			211	Lavender-lt.
149			336	Navy Blue
203			564	Jade-vy. lt.
208			563	Jade-lt.

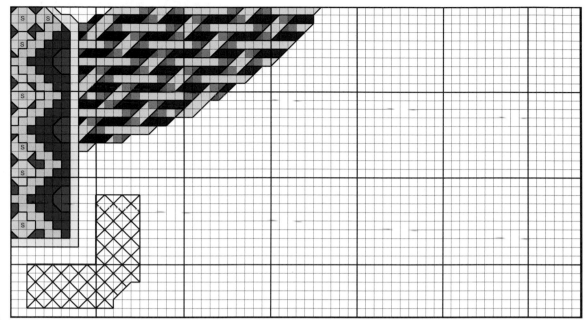

Eternal Life   Bottom Right

255	□ ◿	907	Parrot Green-lt.
258	■ ◿	904	Parrot Green-vy. dk.
387	⊞ ◿	822	Beige Gray-lt.
324	▨ ◿	922	Copper-lt.
349	◹	921	Copper
341	■	919	Red Copper
363	□ ◿	436	Tan

370	▨ ◿	434	Brown-lt.
371	■ ◿	433	Brown-med.
382	■ ◣	3371	Black Brown

Step 2: Backstitch (1 strand)

| 403 | └─┐ | 310 | Black |

SACRED BEASTS

Stitched on amber linen 32 over 2 threads, the finished design size is 7¾" x 9½". The fabric was cut 14" x 16".

Fabric	Design Size
Aida 11	11⅜" x 13⅞"
Aida 14	8⅞" x 10⅞"
Aida 18	7" x 8½"
Hardanger	5⅝" x 7"

Stitch count: 125 x 153

Lord of the animals, Cernunnos was the guardian of the gateway to the underworld. A hunter, he controlled the forces which give and take life through selection and sacrifice in nature.

Anchor			DMC	(used for sample)

Step 1: Cross-stitch (2 strands)

Anchor			DMC	Name		Anchor			DMC	Name
1	·	◿		White		159	▫	◿	3325	Baby Blue-lt.
886	⊠	◿	677	Old Gold-vy. lt.		145	◼	◿	334	Baby Blue-med.
891	▢	◿	676	Old Gold-lt.		147	◼	◿	312	Navy Blue-lt.
890	◼	◿	729	Old Gold-med.		133	S	◿	796	Royal Blue-dk.
301	▫	◿	744	Yellow-pale		256	◼	◿	906	Parrot Green-med.
297	+	◿	743	Yellow-med.		206	▱	◿	955	Nile Green-lt.
303	▩	◿	742	Tangerine-lt.		209	★	◿	913	Nile Green-med.
316	❖	◿	740	Tangerine		205	◼	◿	911	Emerald Green-med.
323	◼	◿	722	Orange Spice-lt.		203	▢	◿	564	Jade-vy. lt.
326	◼	◿	720	Orange Spice-dk.		208	N	◿	563	Jade-lt.
11	◙	◿	350	Coral-med.		210	◼	◿	562	Jade-med.
46	◼	◿	666	Christmas Red-bright		212	◼	◿	561	Jade-vy. dk.
22	◼	◿	816	Garnet		387	Z	◿	822	Beige Gray-lt.
271	▫	◿	3713	Salmon-vy. lt.		830	▢	◿	644	Beige Gray-med.
25	▨	◿	3326	Rose-lt.		392	◼	◿	642	Beige Gray-dk.
27	U	◿	899	Rose-med.		885	◁	◿	739	Tan-ultra vy. lt.
42	◼	◿	335	Rose		362	▢	◿	437	Tan-lt.
85	◼	◿	3609	Plum-ultra lt.		309	◼	◿	435	Brown-vy. lt.
87	◼	◿	3607	Plum-lt.		371	◼	◿	433	Brown-med.
89	◼		917	Plum-med.		403	◼	◿	310	Black
95	◼	◿	554	Violet-lt.						
98	E	◿	553	Violet-med.						
99	◼	◿	552	Violet-dk.						
158	▫	◿	775	Baby Blue-vy. lt.						

Step 2: Backstitch (1 strand)

403	⌐	310	Black

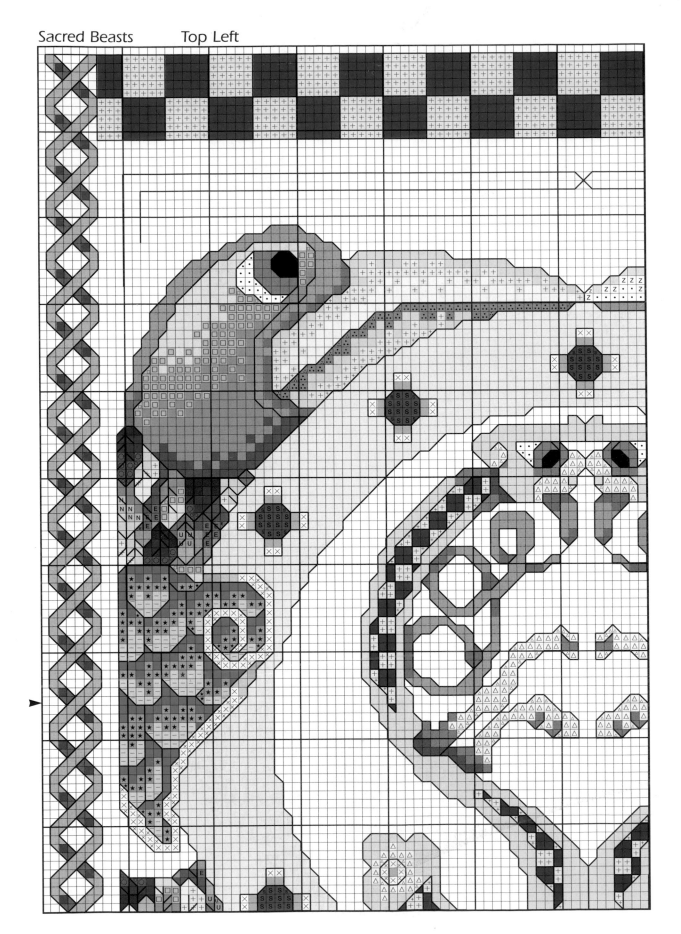

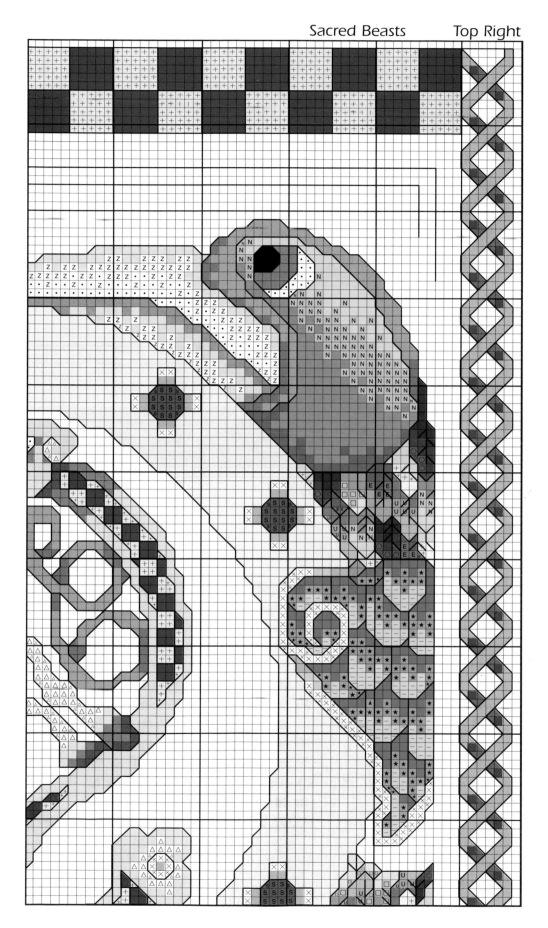

THE STAG

Stitched on antique white Cashel linen 28 over 2 threads, the finished design size is 10" x 11⅜". The fabric was cut 16" x 18".

Fabric	Design Size
Aida 11	12¾" x 14½"
Aida 18	7¾" x 8⅞"
Hardanger	6⅜" x 7¼"

Stitch count: 140 x 160

Associated with Cernnunos, the horned god, the stag represented the wild and untamable nature that is often reflective of man. The stag was praised for its majestic presence and its antlers, which are used for fighting and gaining domination.

Anchor			DMC	(used for sample)
Step 1:			Cross-stitch (2 strands)	
886	□	◿	677	Old Gold-vy. lt.
891	⊟	◿	676	Old Gold-lt.
297	□	◿	743	Yellow-med.
303	⊡	◿	742	Tangerine-lt.
11	■	◢	350	Coral-med.
46	■	◢	666	Christmas Red-bright
25	▨	◿	3326	Rose-lt.
42	◙	◢	335	Rose
22	■	◢	816	Garnet
44	■	◢	814	Garnet-dk.
85	▨	◿	3609	Plum-ultra lt.
87	■		3607	Plum-lt.
89	■		917	Plum-med.
158	□	◿	775	Baby Blue-vy. lt.
159	⊞	◿	3325	Baby Blue-lt.
145	▨	◢	334	Baby Blue-med.
147	■		312	Navy Blue-lt.
149	■		336	Navy Blue
185	◺		964	Seagreen-lt.
213	□	◿	369	Pistachio Green-vy. lt.
206	⊠	◿	564	Jade-vy. lt.
208	▨		563	Jade-lt.
210	Ε		562	Jade-med.

Anchor			DMC	(used for sample)
203	▣	◿	954	Nile Green
204	■		912	Emerald Green-lt.
228	■	◢	910	Emerald Green-dk.
255	▨	◿	907	Parrot Green-lt.
256	S	◿	906	Parrot Green-med.
258	■	◢	904	Parrot Green-vy. dk.
265	□	◿	3348	Yellow Green-lt.
266	W	◿	3347	Yellow Green-med.
268	■	◢	3345	Hunter Green-dk.
387	U	◿	822	Beige Gray-lt.
942	▨	◿	738	Tan-vy. lt.
362	K	◿	437	Tan-lt.
309	■	◢	435	Brown-vy. lt.
371	■	◢	433	Brown-med.
830	□	◿	644	Beige Gray-med.
403	■		310	Black

Step 2: Backstitch (1 strand)

403	⌐	310	Black

Step 3: French Knot (1 strand)

403	●	310	Black

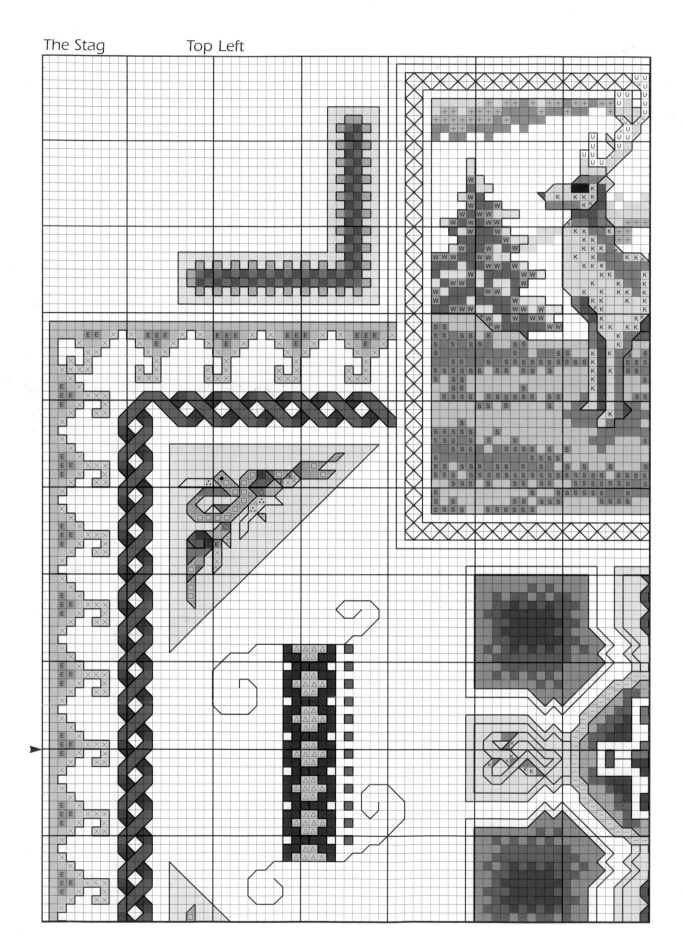

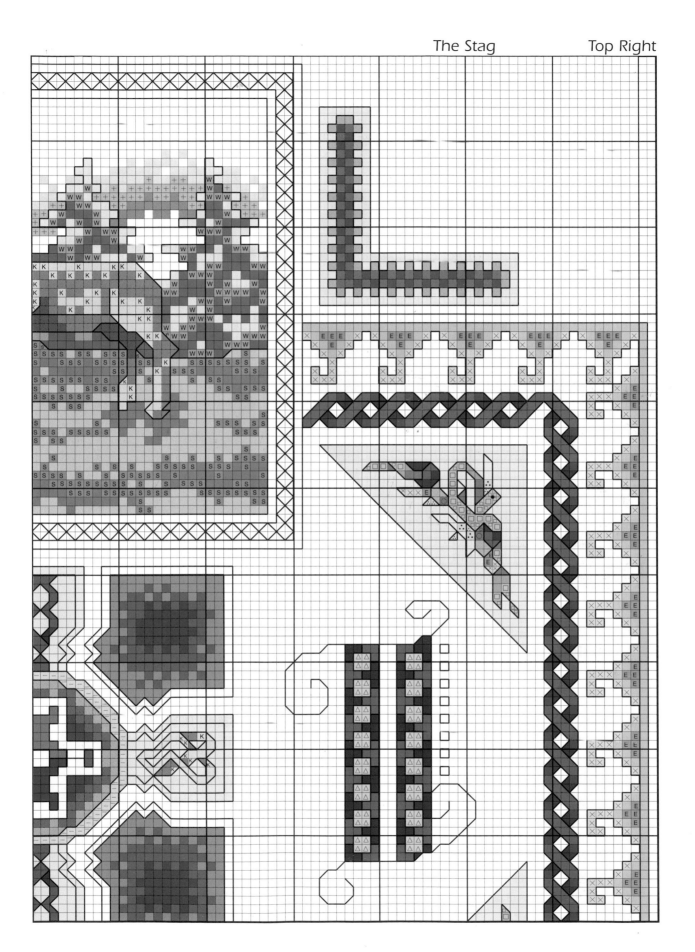

chieftains

Stitched on antique white Cashel linen 28 over 2 threads, the finished design size is 7¼" x 13⅝". The fabric was cut 14" x 20".

Fabric	Design Size
Aida 11	9⅛" x 17¼"
Aida 18	5⅝" x 10½"
Hardanger 22	4⅝" x 8⅝"

Stitch count: 101 x 190

The nobles of Celtic society were known as chieftains. They enjoyed the privilege of owning land. A thriving economy was built on farming and raising cattle, pigs, sheep, and horses.

The assessment of personal worth and dignity was called the "honor price." This price was subject to adjustment according to a person's own fortunes.

It is interesting to note that Celtic women could also inherit properties, occupy positions of high authority and receive an equal division of property of that which is combined from the husband and the wife at the time of marriage.

Anchor			DMC	(used for sample)

Step 1: Cross-stitch (2 strands)

Anchor			DMC	
886	□	◿	677	Old Gold-vy. lt.
891	⊞	◿	676	Old Gold-lt.
890	▥	◿	729	Old Gold-med.
295	□	◿	726	Topaz-lt.
306	◮	◿	725	Topaz
307	▥	◿	783	Christmas Gold
297	□	◹	743	Yellow-med.
303	B	◿	742	Tangerine-lt.
778	·	◿	948	Peach-vy. lt.
8	⊟	◿	353	Peach
316	▥	◿	970	Pumpkin-lt.
330	■	◢	947	Burnt Orange
333	■	◿	900	Burnt Orange-dk.
25	▥	◿	3326	Rose-lt.
27	◉	◿	899	Rose-med.
42	■	◿	335	Rose
46	■	◢	666	Christmas Red-bright
47	▦	◿	304	Christmas Red-med.
43	■	◿	815	Garnet-med.
87	■	◿	3607	Plum-lt.
158	□	◿	775	Baby Blue-vy. lt.
159	▢	◿	3325	Baby Blue-lt.
145	▥	◿	334	Baby Blue-med.
147	■	◹	312	Navy Blue-lt.
185	N	◿	964	Seagreen-lt.
264	□	◿	472	Avocado Green-ultra lt.
266	E	◿	471	Avocado Green-vy. lt.
267	▥	◿	470	Avocado Green-lt.
203	□	◿	564	Jade-vy. lt.
208	M	◿	563	Jade-lt.
210	▥	◿	562	Jade-med.
209	⊠	◿	913	Nile Green-med.
205	▥	◿	911	Emerald Green-med.
229	★	◿	909	Emerald Green-vy. dk.
309	▥	◿	435	Brown-vy. lt.
371	U	◿	433	Brown-med.

Step 2: Backstitch (1 strand)

47	⌐	304	Christmas Red-med.
403	⌐	310	Black

Step 3: French Knot (1 strand)

403	●	310	Black

121

GENERAL INSTRUCTIONS

Fabric for Cross-stitch

Counted cross-stitch is usually worked on even-weave fabrics. These fabrics are manufactured specifically for counted-thread embroidery and are woven with the same number of vertical as horizontal threads per inch. Because the number of threads in the fabric is equal in each direction, each stitch will be the same size. The number of threads per inch in even-weave fabrics determines the size of a finished design. Fabrics used for models are identified in sample information by color, name, and thread count per inch.

Number of Strands

The number of strands used per stitch varies depending on the fabric used. Generally, the rule to follow for cross-stitching is 3 strands on Aida 11, 2 strands on Aida 14, 1 or 2 strands on Aida 18 (depending on desired thickness of stitches) and 1 strand on Hardanger 22. For backstitching, use 1 strand on all fabrics. When completing a french knot, use 2 strands and 1 wrap on all fabrics.

Preparing Fabric

Cut fabric at least 3" larger on all sides than finished design size or cut as indicated in sample information to ensure enough space for project assembly. A 3" margin is the minimum amount of space that allows for comfortably finishing the edges of the design. To prevent fraying, whipstitch or machine-zigzag along raw edges or apply liquid fray preventer.

Needles for Cross-stitch

Needles should slip easily through fabric holes without piercing fabric threads. For fabric with 11 or fewer threads per inch, use a tapestry needle size 24; for 14 threads per inch, use a tapestry needle size 24 or 26; for 18 or more threads per inch, use a tapestry needle size 26. Never leave needle in design area of fabric. It may leave rust or permanent impression on fabric.

Floss

All numbers and color names are cross-referenced between Anchor and DMC brands of floss. Use 18" lengths of floss. For best coverage, separate strands. Dampen with wet sponge. Then put together number of strands called for in color code.

Centering the Design

Fold the fabric in half horizontally, then vertically. Place a pin in the fold point to mark the center. Locate the center of the design on the graph by following the vertical and horizontal arrows in the left and bottom margins. Begin stitching all designs at the center point of graph and fabric, unless the instructions indicate otherwise.

Securing the Floss

Insert needle up from the underside of the fabric at starting point. Hold 1" of thread behind the fabric and stitch over it, securing with the first few stitches. To finish thread, run under four or more stitches on the back of the design. Never knot floss, unless working on clothing. Another method of securing floss is the waste knot. Knot floss and insert needle from the right side of the fabric about 1" from design area. Work several stitches over the thread to secure. Cut off the knot later.

Carrying Floss

To carry floss, weave floss under the previously worked stitches on the back. Do not carry thread across any fabric that is not or will not be stitched. Loose threads, especially dark ones, will show through the fabric.

Cleaning Completed Work

When stitching is complete, soak it in cold water with a mild soap for five to 10 minutes. Rinse well and roll in a towel to remove excess water. Do not wring. Place work face down on a dry towel and iron on warm setting until dry.

Cross-stitch

Stitches are done in a row or, if necessary, one at a time in an area. Stitching is done by coming up through a hole between woven threads at A. Then, go down at B, the hole diagonally across from A. Come back up at C and down at D, etc. Complete the top stitches to create an "X". All top stitches should lie in the same direction. Come up at E and go down at B, come up at C and go down at F, etc.

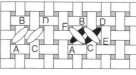

Then, come back up at C. Now, go down one opening to the right, this time at "A".

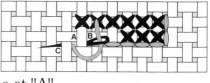

Backstitch

Pull the needle through at the point marked A. Then go down one opening to the right, at B.

French Knot

Bring needle up at A, using two strands of embroidery floss. Loosely wrap floss once around needle. Place needle at B, next to A. Pull floss taut as you push needle down through fabric. Carry floss across back of work between knots.

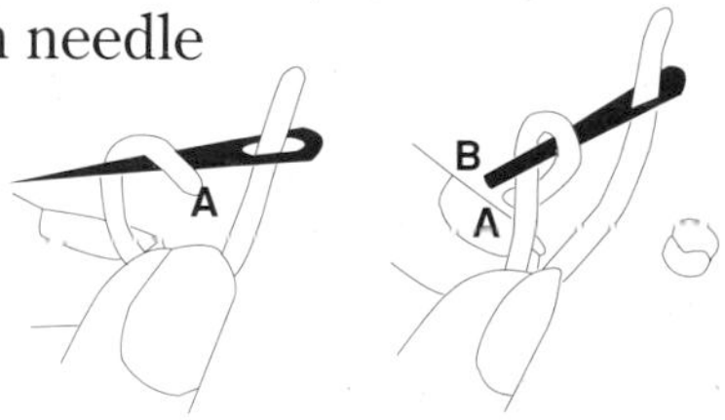

METRIC EQUIVALENCY

MM-Millimetres   CM-Centimetres

INCHES TO MILLIMETRES AND CENTIMETRES

INCHES	MM	CM	INCHES	CM	INCHES	CM
⅛	3	0.3	9	22.9	30	76.2
¼	6	0.6	10	25.4	31	78.7
½	13	1.3	12	30.5	33	83.8
⅝	16	1.6	13	33.0	34	86.4
¾	19	1.9	14	35.6	35	88.9
⅞	22	2.2	15	38.1	36	91.4
1	25	2.5	16	40.6	37	94.0
1¼	32	3.2	17	43.2	38	96.5
1½	38	3.8	18	45.7	39	99.1
1¾	44	4.4	19	48.3	40	101.6
2	51	5.1	20	50.8	41	104.1
2½	64	6.4	21	53.3	42	106.7
3	76	7.6	22	55.9	43	109.2
3½	89	8.9	23	58.4	44	111.8
4	102	10.2	24	61.0	45	114.3
4½	114	11.4	25	63.5	46	116.8
5	127	12.7	26	66.0	47	119.4
6	152	15.2	27	68.6	48	121.9
7	178	17.8	28	71.1	49	124.5
8	203	20.3	29	73.7	50	127.0

YARDS TO METRES

YARDS	METRES	YARDS	METRES	YARDS	METRES	YARDS	METRES	YARDS	METRES
⅛	0.11	2⅛	1.94	4⅛	3.77	6⅛	5.60	8⅛	7.43
¼	0.23	2¼	2.06	4¼	3.89	6¼	5.72	8¼	7.54
⅜	0.34	2⅜	2.17	4⅜	4.00	6⅜	5.83	8⅜	7.66
½	0.46	2½	2.29	4½	4.11	6½	5.94	8½	7.77
⅝	0.57	2⅝	2.40	4⅝	4.23	6⅝	6.06	8⅝	7.89
¾	0.69	2¾	2.51	4¾	4.34	6¾	6.17	8¾	8.00
⅞	0.80	2⅞	2.63	4⅞	4.46	6⅞	6.29	8⅞	8.12
1	0.91	3	2.74	5	4.57	7	6.40	9	8.23
1⅛	1.03	3⅛	2.86	5⅛	4.69	7⅛	6.52	9⅛	8.34
1¼	1.14	3¼	2.97	5¼	4.80	7¼	6.63	9¼	8.46
1⅜	1.26	3⅜	3.09	5⅜	4.91	7⅜	6.74	9⅜	8.57
1½	1.37	3½	3.20	5½	5.03	7½	6.86	9½	8.69
1⅝	1.49	3⅝	3.31	5⅝	5.14	7⅝	6.97	9⅝	8.80
1¾	1.60	3¾	3.43	5¾	5.26	7¾	7.09	9¾	8.92
1⅞	1.71	3⅞	3.54	5⅞	5.37	7⅞	7.20	9⅞	9.03
2	1.83	4	3.66	6	5.49	8	7.32	10	9.14

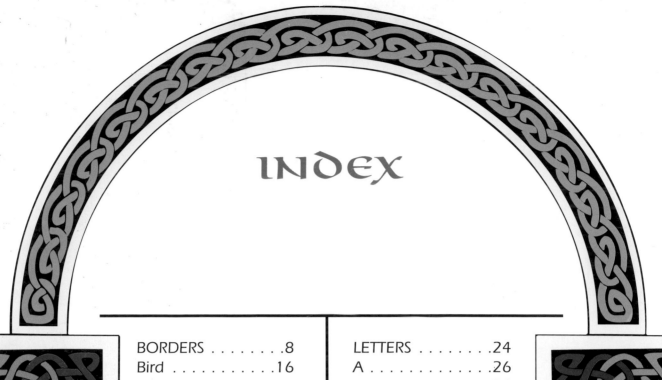

INDEX

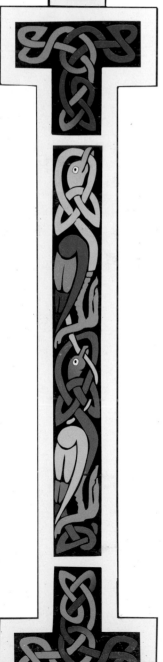